WINGS OVER WATER

In memory of Greg Poole (1960-2018), who thrilled us with his unique interpretations of the natural world and inspired a new generation of wildlife artists

MADE IN NORFOLK BY MASCOT MEDIA

Published in Great Britain in 2019
by Mascot Media, Norfolk, UK.
Email: mascot_media@btinternet.com
www.mascotmedia.co.uk

© 2019 Mascot Media Ltd

A CIP catalogue record for this book is
available from the British Library.

ISBN: 978-1-9164783-1-2

Written and designed by Alan Marshall.
Edited by Marion Scott Marshall.

Printed by Swallowtail Print, Drayton Industrial Park,
Taverham Road, Drayton, Norwich, Norfolk NR8 6RL.
Email: contact@swallowtailprint.co.uk
www.swallowtailprint.co.uk

FSC
www.fsc.org
MIX
Paper from
responsible sources
FSC® C113523

*CAPTIONS Front cover artists, top row, from left: Hugh Ribbans; Lisa
Hooper; Jeremy James; Stuart Brocklehurst. Second row: Ian MacCulloch;
Robert Gillmor; Thelma Sykes; Mike Smith. Third row: Robert Greenhalf.
Bottom row: Richard Jarvis; Chris Sinden; Nick Wonham; Jackie Curtis; Jane
Smith. Back cover artists, top row, from left: Richard Allen; Julia Manning;
Richard Jarvis; Andy English; Greta Hansen. Middle row: Stuart Brocklehurst;
Robert Greenhalf; Greg Poole; Michael Webb. Bottom
row: Rob Barnes; Andrew Haslen; Kittie Jones.
Endpapers: Robert Greenhalf – adapted from
'Minsmere Memories'.*

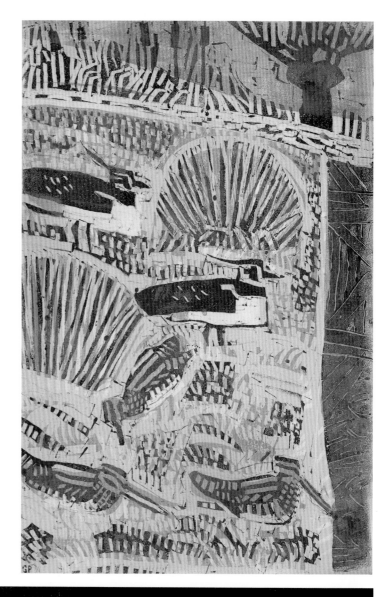

*CAPTIONS
Title page: Arctic Terns and Ringed Plover – Greg Poole
(monoprint), from author's collection. Above: Lapwings and Snipe –
Greg Poole (monoprint), from author's collection.
Left: Halcyon (detail) – Andrew Haslen (linocut). Facing page, top
right: Big Turns and Little Terns III – Carry Akroyd (serigraph).
Bottom right: A Bit of Ruff – Greta Hansen (linocut).
Bottom: Brooding Ringed Plover – Robert Gillmor (linocut).
Page heading motif is based on 'Learg Dubh', a Black-throated
Diver linocut by Lisa Hooper.*

CONTENTS

We have a surprisingly close relationship with water birds. Perhaps, as an island race, our fascination with the sea around us acts as a magnet during weekends and holidays, providing us from an early age with exposure to the gregarious gulls that congregate on the railings and rooftops of our seaside towns.

The practice of feeding ducks and swans with unsuitable crusts at the local pond is also a tradition with deep roots, taking us from extreme youth to extreme old age without any apparent wavering of enthusiasm. Toddlers and the long-retired seem equally keen to indulge the appetite of Mallards and mongrel ducks for surplus baked goods.

Everybody is charmed by the bejewelled Kingfisher when glimpsed perched at the water's edge or, more likely, flashing across the water and flaunting briefly its glorious colours. Most people will never see one, but nonetheless long for the chance.

Without trying too hard, many of us have acquired a knowledge of water-loving bird species, recognising the carrot-billed Oystercatcher probing the mud, or the Cormorant drying its wings like a huge inverted bat.

Water birds have long been employed by artists as a form of adornment in paintings and prints of landscapes, seascapes, etc. Skeins of geese will often trace a path through cloud or across blue skies; flocks of gulls augment coastal or even farming scenes.

The birds themselves began increasingly to be the main subject during the Victorian era. The age of exploration brought home physical or sketched examples of new species, while an increased appetite for scientific knowledge meant that the likes of Thomas Bewick could entertain and inform with his detailed wood engravings that introduced many species to the masses. Andy English and Peter Brown are among those here who continue Bewick's tradition, but with perhaps greater emphasis on art instead of pure illustration.

This book fails spectacularly as a belated sequel to *Bewick's British Birds* but does pay a form of tribute, as we attempt to blend the informative with the decorative. The list of species appearing here is far from exhaustive, and *Wings Over Water* isn't going to replace your well-thumbed field guide. What it aims to do is celebrate the rich diversity of water birds and showcase the great variety of printmaking skills on show in Britain.

Mascot Media's previous titles have campaigned to raise the profile of contemporary printmakers by the use of themes, and this book is in part a companion to our collection of owl prints in *The Elegant Fowl*. As became apparent with that volume and our much-loved *The Artful Hare* and *The Printmaker's Cat*, people love to see the astonishing variety of artistic interpretations of the same subject. As a result, we have this time adopted a somewhat different approach.

In order that readers can compare and contrast 16 depictions of the Avocet and Lapwing, or more than 20 of the Oystercatcher, the book has been arranged alphabetically by species or, occasionally, by bird group – thus breaking our tradition of artist-by-artist presentation.

Some liberties have been taken, and the selection of species is arbitrary and down to the submissions of the artists rather than at the request of the publisher. We have grouped together the gulls, grebes, plovers, divers, etc, to benefit the book design.

If your favourite bird is missing, we apologise. An original print probably exists out there somewhere, but we could never have found the space for every print made

of every bird that has a direct connection with freshwater or saltwater habitat.

The narrative running through *Wings Over Water* makes the link between the bird species, conservation status, distribution and habits with its choice as a subject by one or more artists. The printmakers have been given the chance to explain their love for a particular bird; describe the circumstances in which the image was conceived; and detail the process used. Given the precarious state of so many species, we hope that the text also provides a wake-up call for those unaware of how threatened some of these birds have become.

Some 50 artists have work reproduced in this book, mostly living and working in the UK. In a handful of cases, the author and his wife have raided their own extensive collection of wildlife art to show examples. The majority of the images have, however, been supplied by the printmakers themselves.

Some of you will have noticed the dedication that appears on the opening page. Between the start of this project in the autumn of 2018 and its completion in the spring of 2019, we lost a remarkably talented and influential artist by the name of Greg Poole, based in Bristol, who passed away far too young but still leaves a great legacy of much-admired and highly original work.

Greg had supported our earlier titles with some outstanding contributions, and by way of small tribute we have reproduced in this book a couple of our own prints representing wonderful interpretations of water birds.

The range of printmaking skills on show throughout the book is considerable. Wood engravings and woodcuts sit side by side with collagraphs and linocuts. The one-off monoprints and monotypes share space with screenprints. There are some newer processes and several prints produced using a combination of traditional methods.

While the offset litho printing of this book inserts another degree of separation between the artists' original blocks and the reader, these pages aim to be faithful representations of original prints, not of photo-mechanical copies of paintings or drawings.

Printmaking requires the observational skills shared by all artists, as well as the imagination to translate a visual impression into a two-dimensional artwork. It generally calls on the ability to record those first impressions in pencil or ink, before the more craft-based stages of carving wood or lino, cutting shapes and etching metal transform the idea into an object to be inked and printed on to beautiful paper. The resulting print is an original in its own right, often varying slightly within small editions sold at an affordable price that brings fine art within the reach of almost everyone.

As ever, we express our gratitude to those who have contributed images and words. We take full responsibility for the way in which we have reproduced, arranged, edited and rewritten in order to create *Wings Over Water*. We share a love of the subject matter and the processes involved, and hope that this collection inspires others either to appreciate the birds more fully, buy the art or take up printmaking themselves.

Alan Marshall
Sutton, Norfolk, March 2019.

From left to right: Black-tailed Godwit – John Tennant (screenprint, from author's collection); Cley Marshes, Norfolk, April 1969 – Robert Hainard (woodcut – from author's collection); Tideline Foragers – Valerie Sims (woodcut); A Family Outing, Swinsty Reservoir – Mike Smith (linocut); Mandarin Duck – Peter Brown (wood engraving).

ARTISTS

From left: Muscovy Ducks, 1951 – Clifford Webb (linocut, from author's collection); Wells Before Dark – Max Angus (linocut); Storm Petrel – Richard Allen (linocut); Turnstones – Robert Gillmor (linocut); Salthouse Wigeon – Max Angus (linocut). Pages 8-9: 18 linocut prints from 'Coastal Birds' by Richard Allen.

Avocet

Below: Brooding Avocet – Robert Gillmor (linocut). Right: Minsmere – Richard Allen (linocut).
Facing page: Four Avocet – Robert Greenhalf (woodcut). *Overleaf.* P12, top: An Orchestra of Avocets –
Julie Orpen (linocut). P12, bottom: Avocet Rest – John Hatton (linocut). P13: Feeding Frenzy –
Lisa Hooper (linocut).

An orchestra of Avocets

FEW BIRD-MINDED PRINTMAKERS spurn the opportunity to tackle an Avocet at some point in their career. Robert Gillmor admits to being a serial Avocet linocutter, and in 2018 produced the latest in a long line of prints – this time to celebrate his appearance on *BBC Springwatch*.

It is easy to see from this collection of images why the birds appeal. Not only do they boast elegance and grace, but the upturned bill and contrasting black/white plumage make for a very pleasing combination.

The unique beak isn't, of course, a quirky design aimed at entertaining artists. These surprisingly belligerent birds sweep their down-turned heads through the water in arcs, just above the surface of the mud, as they search for invertebrates. They can be bullies, chasing off other waders and wildfowl on their patch. They are, however, undeniably beautiful.

Avocets are a conservation triumph, to the extent that their appearance as the RSPB logo is deemed by many to be inappropriate. Their future in the UK appears to have been secured, with an estimated 1,500 breeding pairs. Between 7,000 and 8,000 birds over-winter in Britain – a remarkable turnaround from near-extinction 80 years ago.

Before and after the breeding season, Avocets can be found in groups of 6-30 birds. Less common are the large feeding flocks that can number in the hundreds. During breeding season, the flocks dissipate. Summer groups can be large, comprising immature non-breeding birds joined later by failed breeders and some adults with fledged young.

While conservation status has improved greatly in the UK, the Avocet remains on the Amber list to reflect its localised distribution in Britain and Europe. Most of the British birds nest

within reserves, where habitat is managed carefully by the RSPB and by other bodies. It would be all too easy to allow habitat loss to once again jeopardise the species.

Prints by Richard Allen and Robert Gillmor open this section, with the former one of many current artists grateful to the latter for inspiration and support. Robert's 'Brooding Avocet' linocut on page 10 was based "almost precisely on a quite finished drawing of a bird that was nesting close to the

hide at RSPB Titchwell. It is not often that I make use of sketches in this way. Usually they end up being referred to, in order to construct compositions not so closely based on direct observation. I like to find the decorative possibilities in a group of birds where their plumage patterns combine to produce a satisfactory overall design. This often brings me back to species with bold areas of colour, or solely dark and light."

Given that the Avocet began its recovery in

coastal East Anglia, and the region now hosts a large population, a number of the contributing artists spotted the birds behind their designs in Suffolk and Norfolk. Jeremy James (page 18, middle) describes the Avocet as "an elegant, beautiful bird that always looks far too exotic for an East Anglian wetland!".

Suffolk-based Julie Orpen, responsible both for the collective noun and Avocet print on page 12, selected the title as it suits so well the beautiful surroundings of the concert hall

Top left: Avocets – Caroline Barker (linocut). Top right: Rummaging in the Reeds – Greta Hansen (collagraph). Left: Springwatch Avocets – Robert Gillmor (linocut). Opposite: Avocets – Kerry Buck (collagraph).

at Snape Maltings near Aldeburgh, where she has often enjoyed watching the birds.

While Scottish Borders-based artist Lisa Hooper is located hundreds of miles from East Anglia, her hand-coloured linocut 'Feeding Frenzy' on page 13 was inspired by Avocets in north Norfolk. "They are such beautiful birds (although much maligned by birdwatchers because of their aggressive behaviour and perhaps always seen as interlopers): every printmaker has to have a go at them! In this case the reflections of

the birds in the water are crucial to the design and lend an oriental quality to the print.

"When I first moved to Scotland I made a series of large prints on to coloured paper which were then hand coloured. Necessity was the mother of invention because for many years I only had an etching press which made it difficult to register print from more than one plate (in different colours). My press was only really good for one pass, so I started out by hand colouring, and the use of coloured paper was a way of introducing

another colour. The prints were coloured using water-based poster paints that are repelled by the oil-based inks. Because an etching press was used, the paper was consequently quite deeply embossed."

Nick Wonham's 'Feeding Avocet' above is another linocut inspired by a visit to RSPB Titchwell in north Norfolk. "The Avocet is the perfect subject matter for the printmaker. As with the Oystercatcher, the black and white plumage lends itself to being portrayed as a linocut."

Richard Allen's opening linocut of Avocets is quite clearly based at Suffolk's RSPB Minsmere, the spiritual home of the species. The cottages at nearby Dunwich Heath can be seen in the background, as can a

Left: Avocets – Glynn Thomas (etching). Above: Avocets –
Jeremy James (linocut). Right: Preening Avocets –
Robert Greenhalf (woodcut).

Marsh Harrier, another Minsmere speciality.

Suffolk printmaker Glynn Thomas was on location at Norfolk's Cley-next-the-Sea when producing his etching of Avocets (facing page) – note the famous windmill in the background. Greta Hansen, another Suffolk artist, captures Avocets in her collagraph 'Rummaging in the Reeds' on page 14 and in the woodcut 'Low Tide' on page 17.

Andrew Haslen, again based in Suffolk,

has turned recently to multi-block linocuts and a more subdued colour palette for his printmaking. An early example is the 'Resting Avocet' on page 16. He finds inspiration for his work on his home patch, while Sussex-based Robert Greenhalf had to travel rather farther to capture ideas for his Avocet woodcuts at Minsmere and in Norfolk (page 11 and above) – although there is plenty of nature on his south-eastern doorstep.

For John Hatton, the linocut on page 12 portrays the Avocet in another familiar pose, standing on one leg with head tucked in during a daytime nap – but with a wary eye ready to open at the first hint of trouble.

Caroline Barker sees the Avocets that inspired her linocut on page 14 on her local south Devon estuary or at the Slimbridge reserve in Gloucestershire. "To paraphrase Gerard Manley Hopkins, a Pied Beauty."

BARNACLE GOOSE

AT A DISTANCE, IN FLIGHT, this largely two-tone bird can be confused with the Brent Goose, but has longer wings and flaps more slowly while making the journey (with more than 100,000 of its companions) from Svalbard or Greenland to its UK wintering grounds on the Solway Firth. John Hatton on the right captures the character of these birds with their "blue-grey barred backs", while Nick Wonham provided the vinyl cut print at the top of the page. "The little vignette of a Barnacle Goose was executed in a slightly different style after I'd just bought my first Pfeil linocutting tools," explains Nick. "I couldn't resist putting in a bit more detail. I ran off a few copies of this print as Christmas presents for my amazing class team that I work alongside at a special needs school in north London, as a thank-you for all their hard work."

Top right: Barnacle Goose – Nick Wonham (vinyl cut). Right: Barnacle Trio – John Hatton (linocut).

BEARDED TIT

APOLOGIES TO THOSE WHO PREFER 'Bearded Reedling', but these charming birds are known to most of us as Bearded Tits (no relation to genuine Titmice). Robert Greenhalf here captures them twice in woodcut form. "Notoriously difficult to see, these were sketched on a very rough day at Stodmarsh in Kent when they performed right in front of me, clinging to the violently swaying stems for several minutes." Robert's print 'Minsmere Memories' is a compilation of images from sketches and more finished paintings and prints made during several visits to the Suffolk reserve.

With a summer population barely above 600 pairs, Bearded Tits can be a rare sighting away from strongholds in coastal Norfolk and Suffolk, stretches of the south coast and a perhaps surprising colony on Scotland's River Tay in Perth and Kinross. While conservation status puts the bird on the Green list, numbers can fluctuate wildly.

Below: Minsmere Memories –
Robert Greenhalf (woodcut).
Right: Bearded Tits –
Robert Greenhalf (woodcut).

BITTERN

ONE OF THE MANY FAMILIAR NAMES FOR THE Bittern is 'Bull o' the Bog', and this title is attached to Robert Gillmor's striking 2012 linocut opposite.

Wood engraver Andy English admits that he has heard Bitterns much more often than he has seen them. "It is years since I caught a glimpse of these secretive birds. They are so well disguised that I decided to engrave a pair with one of them hidden in the reeds." Look closely at the wonderful print below and you'll spot them both!

The author is spoiled in that, living in the Norfolk Broads, the opportunity exists for relatively regular sightings of this elusive species. While crossing Hickling Broad, they can be spotted overhead with their distinctive flight and shape, standing still among the reeds on the hunt for fish and frogs, or striding slowly but purposefully from one sheltered spot to another.

According to BTO data, there are only 80 males to

be seen nationwide during the summer, so any spot is always a thrill. During the winter, there can be upwards of 600 birds in Britain. The Bittern is Amber listed but doing rather better than a decade ago. Programmes to re-establish wetland habitats in the UK can only help the population and give more people a chance to see (or at least hear) one of the bird world's true characters.

On the facing page, in Jeremy James' hand-coloured linocut, birdwatchers may have heard a booming from the hide, but share the frustration of seeing absolutely no evidence of the bird. Norfolk-based artist Deborah Vass on page 24 shows the brief glimpse that many of us catch as the

Left: Bitterns – Andy English (wood engraving). Far left: Minsmere Bittern – Jeremy James (linocut). Right: Bull o' the Bog – Robert Gillmor (linocut).

bird rears up from the reeds.

Mandy Walden is a Suffolk-based printmaker and painter with a taste for the mysterious and atmospheric corners of the county. Her moonlit Bittern collagraph on the left is entitled 'Watching as the Moon Rolls Silently out to Sea', and represents the bird on Minsmere's marshes.

The Bittern's famous booming call, resulting in the Bull o' the Bog' moniker, can carry for more than a kilometre, teasing patient birdwatchers into thinking they may be in for a glimpse. Each bird's call is slightly different, enabling keen-eared scientists to identify each male and help monitor population and breeding success.

While a male may mate with several females on his territory, he has no role in nest-building or maintenance. There is usually just the one brood per year for the female, of five to six eggs.

While little is known about the rearing of the young and success in fledging, there are plenty of predators in the water and among the reeds. Slow but steady population growth suggests that the proportion of chicks reaching adulthood is relatively small.

Above left: Watching as the Moon Rolls Silently out to Sea, Minsmere – Mandy Walden (collagraph). Above right: Bittern – Deborah Vass (linocut).

BRENT GOOSE

Right: Brent Geese in the Morning – Fiona Carver (linocut). Below: watercolour sketch for 'Brent Geese in the Morning'. Below right: rolling ink on to lino block. Page 26, top: Brent Geese – Lisa Hooper (linocut). Page 26, bottom: Brent Geese – Richard Allen (linocut).

THE SMALLEST BRITISH GOOSE, THE BRENT has a nicely contrasting look that can work well as a linocut, as evidenced by these from Fiona Carver, Lisa Hooper and Richard Allen.

Fiona's five-block print was inspired by a cold Easter morning in North Wales. "I looked out across the usually deserted beach and it was covered in Brent Geese. They were busy waddling around, exploring the wet sand. Just for that moment, the beach was all theirs, before anyone else woke up and disturbed the peace. I started by sketching the geese and then decided on a composition. I painted a watercolour sketch and used this to work out the colours and shapes for the linocut."

For Lisa, the geese were the start of a new process involving Apple's iPad Pro. "I intended to use it as an aid to design, and quickly found it invaluable. The drawings I produce on it are for some reason simpler and more playful than anything I can do on paper. It also helps enormously with the early design stages of a print where I previously used tracing paper to move and reverse elements within a composition.

"My first iPad design, this was inspired by Brent Geese in Southampton Water swimming away as I approached them. The simple colour scheme lends itself well to reduction printing."

BUNTINGS

THE REED BUNTING IS TECHNICALLY THE ONLY BIRD IN this section that meets all of this book's inclusion criteria. However, visiting Snow Buntings are seen more often than not on the shore, and inspired Richard Allen's lovely black-and-white linocut (with accompanying sketch) overleaf. While breeding on mountain tops in Greenland and Scandinavia, Snow Buntings winter on sandy and shingle coasts. Richard combines the birds with Sea Kale in his print.

Robert Gillmor in 2007 used the birds as a suitably seasonal subject for a Christmas card and a print, shown on

Left: Reed Bunting – Richard Jarvis (linocut). Below: Reed Bunting – Richard Allen (linocut).

page 28. "We find approachable Snow Buntings each winter on the shingle beach a few minutes from the cottage [in Cley-next-the-Sea]. Their bold black-and-white plumage, with touches of ochre, is perfect for the linocut treatment."

In the case of the Reed Bunting, which the author will often see popping to the tops of Broadland riverside reedbeds as the light slips away, Richard Jarvis, Richard Allen and Robert Gillmor catch them mid-song. The latter artist observes that 'singing' may be too kind a description for the bird's "somewhat repetitive and rusty" call. The drawing below and linocut to the right were worked up from sketches made of a male in the spring at Titchwell.

Richard Jarvis explains that his local counties of Leicestershire, Rutland and Northamptonshire are blessed with many reservoirs of various sizes, along with canals and rivers, all attracting a cast of water-loving species throughout the seasons.

"My favourite canal-side walk near Foxton Locks provides inspiring sightings of all kinds of wildlife, including a Reed Bunting giving his rather simple song from a clump of Reed mace on a March morning [page 27]. For the majority of my prints I use oil-based ink; these are then hand-tinted with watercolour."

Facing page, top: Snow Buntings and Sea Kale – Richard Allen (linocut). Facing page, bottom left: sketch by Richard Allen for Snow Buntings. Facing page, bottom right: Snow Buntings – Robert Gillmor (linocut). Above right: Reed Bunting – Robert Gillmor (linocut). Left: Reed Bunting sketch by Robert Gillmor.

COOT

Top: Scootering – Thelma Sykes (linocut). Above: Cootling – Valerie Sims (woodcut).
Right: Trio of Coots – Sue Brown (collagraph).

GIVEN THE NUMBERS SOMETIMES ENCOUNTERED on open water and along the fringes of rivers and streams, it is hard to believe that the Coot was once persecuted almost to the point of no return. Shooting, nest-raiding for eggs and habitat loss once put huge pressure on the population. Now Green-listed and considered common, these noisy and aggressive birds can be seen throughout the UK – building island nests such as that seen on the left in Valerie Sims' print inspired by an outing to St Ives in Cambridgeshire.

While the white shield above the beak is the key distinguishing feature, providing the basis for the rather unkind 'bald as a coot', the feet are also fascinating – as captured on the right by Sue Brown. The lobed flaps of skin on the toes provide a form of webbing that helps drive the bird through the water while creating significant splashing, as recorded above by Thelma Sykes. It makes for a particularly entertaining show when ice is encountered and the Coot indulge in skating (see overleaf).

Located near the Dee estuary, Thelma Sykes is a veteran field naturalist and printmaker who enjoys greatly the process of composition when preparing her linocuts and woodcuts. "Some of this is intuitive; some calculated. I try to orchestrate the way in which the eye will move around the image. For instance, the western eye reads more readily from left to right, so my skirmishing Coots in 'Scootering' [above] move that way, too.

"The contrast of white bills against dark heads draws the eye, and I set these contrasts at different heights to convey restlessness; the intervals between them are irregular, too, which pulls the eye through the group to the fleeing bird. Then the backward

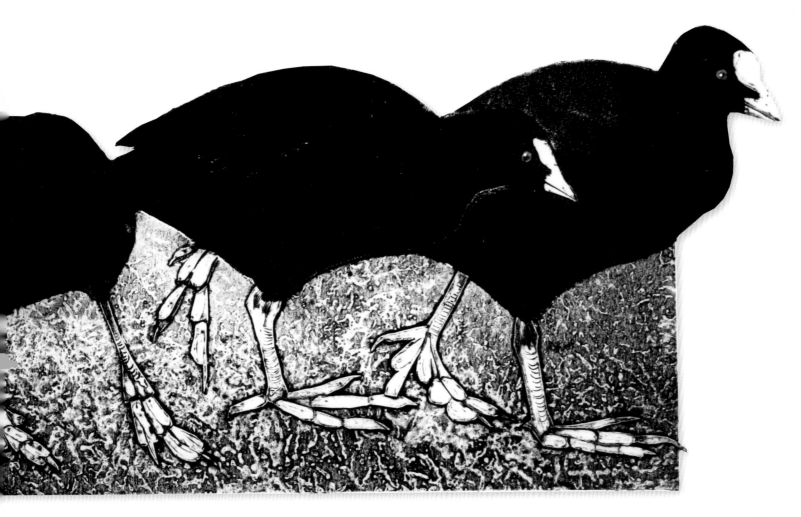

curve of this bird's wing echoes the arc of the splash behind it, and together these return the eye for another run. I want to share the excitement of the moment – oh, yes, and I hope to raise a smile!

"The print is a straightforward one-, two-, three-stage reduction block, printing from light to dark, but I brushed ink from the upraised wings to suggest movement and my registration needed to be spot on through all three printings if the splashes of water showing against the flanks of the coots were to stay crisp."

Looking for all the world like an outtake from the film *March of the Penguins*, the snowy scene at the top of this page acknowledges Thelma's interest in animal behaviour. "This is Ellesmere, Shropshire, on an icy day. I noticed Coots walking in line and staggering their positions so that each bird could see ahead – much as motorists do when stuck in a slow-moving queue of traffic and each driver inches

out closer to the central white line, forming an echelon. The feathering on a Coot's head and nape is short and dense, while that on the rump often stands up in a ruff – and so these areas appear to be darker. It is this punctuation of dark heads and tails that gives the line its movement.

"I wanted this to be an emotive piece with a soft, almost lithographic, quality that would describe the weather. I've 'ragged' over the ink on the block on the underparts of the Coot to show cool light bouncing back from the snow. By changing the pressure and direction of the rag, I established the form of the birds, even defining their outline where the bodies overlapped; it gives soft-edged shapes not usually associated with linocut.

"Whenever I see Coot out of water, I take the opportunity to enjoy those remarkable lobed toes: superbly adapted for swimming as well as for walking – but they make me smile."

The Coot parade through falling snow shown at the bottom of the facing page is a linocut by Jenny Portlock, now living in France and perhaps less often experiencing the weather faced by the birds.

There is also nothing but cold comfort for the Coots in Thelma's final linocut [above] as the birds stand about on their flanged feet waiting for signs of a thaw.

"The cut of the knife and gouge on lino gives the medium its expressive crisp edge that I so enjoy. In 'Frieze', however, I wanted something different to describe that nebulous interface between water and ice, and used the torn edge of heavy printmaking paper as a mask. The soft light and shade on the birds adds further contrast: I achieve this by manipulating the ink on the block before each printing, a monoprint technique repeated for each print in the edition.

"For my final printing, the block was cut to

leave just the heads and rumps; on the Coot these always appear a darker and more velvety feathering. There was so little lino left proud on the block that I hand-burnished this last stage. I always keep my blocks, but the only lino left on this one is a row of part heads and tails."

Thelma's life-long passion for birds began on an estuary, so waders and wildfowl were her first love. "The areas I have returned to time and again include the lochs and rivers of the Cairngorms; the Moray Firth; the coastline of Caithness and sea lochs of Sutherland; then south to the Camel Estuary and Cornwall's north coast; east to The Wash from Snettisham to Cley-next-the-Sea. In all these places I can settle quickly. Then back home to the Dee Estuary; the meres of Cheshire and Shropshire; the Welsh coast; and Anglesey.

"It is for its transformative effects that I love the wet. It takes the animals that live in, on or over it and shape-shifts them as in a flicker book. There are repeating patterns everywhere in nature: my mind is attuned to them, and reflections in water give a pattern double measure. It is the rhythm and the variety that keep my focus, and nothing provides such transitions so well as water."

Top: Snow March – Thelma Sykes (linocut). Above left: Frieze – Thelma Sykes (linocut). Above right, pencil sketch for 'Frieze'. Left: Hurry, it's Snowing – Jenny Portlock (linocut).

CORMORANT

WINGS OVER WATER

THE PHRASE 'HUNG OUT TO DRY' SEEMS purpose-made for the Cormorant, pictured more often than not with drying outspread wings like a large, inverted bat. The absence of essential oils used by other bird species to keep their feathers dry and warm helps provide the Cormorant with fantastic mobility and speed through the water. This, however, requires the regular perching and drying sessions that are beloved of artists.

Given a large population of waterside wind pumps with sails on the Norfolk Broads, the author is often entertained by the sight of Cormorant flocks hogging the vantage points provided by these towering structures. Visiting groups of Cormorants to inland freshwater locations are a mixed blessing for some, but a welcome addition to the landscape for others.

The impressive woodblock on page 35 by Somerset artist Jackie Curtis is a frenzy

of straight-winged flight and feather drying. "I love the distinctive shapes of Cormorants as they hang out together drying their wings while draped on bare branches. There are also lovely strong patterns in their feathers which make them an ideal subject for a linocut or a woodblock. This block is cut from elm which leaves a very strong woodgrain in the print."

Set against a backdrop of sparkling sea, Julia Manning's woodcut print 'Dale of Walls' on page

34 shows silhouetted Cormorant passing the rocks at wave height. The artist observed the flypast during 50mph winds off Shetland in October. Julia, winner of Mascot Media's inaugural 'Wildlife in Print' award at the Society of Wildlife Artists' 2018 Natural Eye Exhibition, makes her ambitious woodcuts using plywood or large planks of coarse wood that bring an element of grain and direction to the resulting print.

Below left is Cambridgeshire artist Nina Sage's brand-new reduction multi-block linocut print completed just in time for inclusion in *Wings Over Water*. A reduction linocut is typically just the one block, carved and printed progressively as more lino is removed. In this instance, the artist has used three blocks, with just one reduced.

Fiona Carver's 'Watching the Waves' linocut below is based on a group of Cormorants she spotted on a small outcrop of rocks in North Wales. "Surrounded by a choppy sea, they seemed completely at ease just watching the waves crashing over their little patch. I'm fascinated by the way water and sea moves, and I

Facing page: Cormorants – Nina Sage (linocut).
Below: Watching the Waves – Fiona Carver (linocut).

wanted to portray the energy of it around the rocks against the slick black feathers of the birds.

"I started by sketching, painting and scribbling the waves with loose, free lines. I transferred these exactly to the lino in order to retain the dynamism of the marks. I wanted the background sea to appear layered, so I mixed my ink with extender to give it a translucency. Again, this adds to the energy of the water."

Anne Townshend's three-block linocut print (below left) is the result of the artist's regular walks along the coast and through the marshland of Suffolk and north Essex, where the birdlife is varied and abundant.

"Bawdsey, at the mouth of the river Deben, is a favourite haunt – it seems so remote and totally peaceful. I sketched the jagged rusty iron sheet of breakwater and mauvey-blue horizon where sea met land. Back in the studio, while I was transferring my sketch to a block, I decided to use a little artistic licence and add the Cormorant drying his wings (which I'd witnessed in a totally different location weeks before!). I used caustic soda on the lino to etch the clouds, achieving a softer effect."

Kent-based Hugh Ribbans ('Water Wings', far right) gives us a feast of water birds, topped by the Cormorant but supported ably by Curlew, Oystercatcher and Egret (among others) in this large and complex linocut. Living on a creek in north Kent, overlooking the marshes and backing on to the Saxon Shore Way, scenes like this are a daily occurrence.

Valerie Sims on the right captures her drying Cormorant near Cuckoo Bridge in Cambridgeshire. The River Great Ouse bypasses the Roswell Pits nature reserve, where the artist may never have seen a Cuckoo but has enjoyed the occasional Kingfisher and plentiful Cormorant, grebes, gulls, Coot, herons and Mallards.

Top left: Cormorant – Janice Earley (linocut). Bottom left: Cormorant – Anne Townshend (linocut). Right: Cormorant – Richard Allen (linocut). Far right: Water Wings – Hugh Ribbans (linocut). Below: Cuckoo Bridge – Valerie Sims (woodcut).

CRANE

Right: Clarion Crane – Robert Gillmor (linocut). Opposite: A Dance of Cranes – Julie Orpen (linocut).

STARTLINGLY EXOTIC AND ALIEN, CRANES never fail to cause a stir as they throw unusual shapes in the sky above, or bugle loudly from the reedbeds. This is a bird many of us might never have expected to see wild in the UK – and many more will probably never see unless they visit a few specific, isolated locations.

Grus grus is nowadays an Amber-listed species with a small breeding population in Norfolk, plus reintroduced birds in Somerset and visitors in the spring and autumn.

Seemingly too big for the UK's wetlands, towering over the Grey Heron, the crane represents an extraordinary sight and sound.

Perhaps 50 pairs now breed in the UK, and another 150 pairs may over-winter on our shores, making this a memorable spot for the birdwatcher and wildlife artist. Cranes returned to breed on the Norfolk Broads in 1981, and the colony at Horsey between Hickling and the north-east coast has become a major birdwatching

location as well as a vital habitat.

Norfolk-based Robert Gillmor is responsible for the linocut print above. "When titling this print, I could not find a distant or romantic name for the Crane, so added 'Clarion' to remind us of its wild, bugling calls. The sexes are indistinguishable as they strut together in display and courtship bonding. There are six printings in this design: two greens for the background reeds, red, yellow, blue and black."

A dance of Cranes

Julie Orpen created her own collective noun, 'A Dance of...', for her linocut (above) that features mating displays rather than recreational cavorting. She, like many East Anglian artists, is grateful for the opportunity to enjoy these extraordinary birds in the wild.

Jackie Curtis (overleaf) is based in Somerset and can now enjoy the full crane experience on her doorstep. "Cranes have recently been reintroduced to the Somerset Levels, and I was lucky enough not only to find a group out there but also to see a 'group huddle' as the Cranes welcomed another group by gathering together – stretching their necks upwards and bugling; almost embracing one another." Jackie's linocut combines the welcoming cranes with flocks of Lapwing, sharing the wetland environment.

East Sussex artist Robert Greenhalf provides the colourful woodcut of Cranes that completes this section, showing the somewhat ungainly sight of the large birds in the air, legs trailing. "Made after a very inspiring visit to the Lac du Der in France where Cranes winter and stop off on their migration north in the spring from Extremadura in Spain to their breeding grounds in Eastern Europe."

The author's first sight of cranes flying over the small Norfolk road passing Horsey windpump almost resulted in a crash, such was his surprise at seeing these wonderful birds passing low over the marshland.

Opposite: Cranes and Lapwings – Jackie Curtis (linocut). Above: Cranes – Robert Greenhalf (woodcut).

CURLEW

THERE IS SOMETHING PARTICULARLY WISTFUL and wild about the Curlew, reflecting its call, distinctive shape and the remote spots it will often frequent. A large wading bird with trademark long, downturned beak shared with the Whimbrel, this wetland species also likes to keep its feet dry in upland habitats. More than 65,000 pairs breed in the UK, but the winter population can often exceed 140,000 birds.

We have a particular responsibility when it comes to Curlew conservation, as almost a third of the western European breeding population can be found in the UK. Sadly, numbers have declined at an alarming rate, falling some 48 per cent between 1995 and 2015. Once again, habitat loss is a major contributor, particularly in the upland areas where the tracts of undisturbed grassland are vanishing fast. The BTO has launched a Curlew Appeal in order to try and reverse the worrying trend.

Yorkshire artist Hester Cox (whose depictions of the bird appear throughout this section) is a champion of the Curlew cause, producing a series of prints capturing the birds in a moorland setting, where they appear to be at greatest risk. "While I often depict birds in my prints, I have a particular love of Curlews and I have made many images of them over the years.

"My obsession began in 2011 when I was one of three artists in residence at a small rural museum 14 miles from where I lived. We were asked to take inspiration from their birds' egg collection, and I fell in love with a beautiful Curlew's egg. This was the starting point for my work, but my cycle ride over the moors to the museum became more significant than the collection itself when I realised that Curlews migrated inland from the west coast to breed there.

"I spent a number of happy days up on the moors observing the birds at close quarters while

Above: Walberswick Curlew – Jeremy James (linocut). Right: Curlew Calling – Richard Jarvis (linocut).

sitting among the heather with the bees humming and the sun on my back. I made sound recordings, sketched them and photographed them in flight. The result of my studies was a series of prints about their migration and the nest sites.

"I now live in a wilder area of the Yorkshire Dales, and we are fortunate to have many Curlews, Lapwings, Golden Plovers and Oystercatchers breeding here. The haunting cry of the Curlew always heralds the imminent arrival of spring for me. In the early summer I often hear them calling in the meadow beyond my studio, and it is a sad day when I realise they have returned to the coast in mid-August.

"One of the most beautiful sights I've seen was a flock of feeding Curlew in swirling snow by the River Cover. The scene was almost completely white apart from a row of thorn trees and the birds themselves."

Lisa Hooper's hand-coloured collagraph of Curlews (page 51) is based on "the large flocks of Curlew that gather on the seaweed just north of St Margaret's Hope on South Ronaldsay, Orkney, in the autumn"; while Julia Manning's 'Returning Tide' woodcut (page 48) portrays the birds in Shetland.

Ysabel Winzar is a painter and printmaker based in south Devon. Her work reflects both

Left: Feeding Curlew – Kittie Jones (monotype). Facing page, top left: The Return – Hester Cox (collagraph). Facing page, top right: Curlew – Richard Allen (linocut). Facing page, bottom: Curlew – Ysabel Winzar (linocut).

Above: Returning Tide – Julia Manning (woodcut).

Above: Curlew Summer – Hester Cox (collagraph).

'Conyer Curlew' (above)

rapid glimpses and concentrated observations from her varied 'stuff of life' which, since childhood, has included art. As a sailor, Ysabel shares the Salcombe estuary with the Curlews that forage on the foreshore of the boatyard where she used to work – an elegant sight amid the bustle of boatyard activity. Her two-plate linocut appears on page 47.

Hugh Ribbans is often distracted by the activity of water birds outside his north Kent window, with the likes of his 'Conyer Curlew' (above) working their way up the creek feeding in the mud at low tide.

'Feeding Curlew', the monotype by Kittie Jones on page 46, won the RSPB Award at the SWLA Natural Eye Exhibition in 2018. "This piece was inspired by memories of a day spent drawing on the soft, pale beach at Tyninghame Estuary in East Lothian. I worked on a large-scale monochrome drawing, crouched on the sand, scribbling in waders feeding along the water's edge and hastily erasing them, leaving a lone Curlew surrounded by shapes of water and land. The Curlew is an elusive bird and therefore difficult to capture – through a series of bold marks I felt I had a feeling for the stoop and curve of its body. The drawing remained on my studio wall for some time before I decided to try it as a monotype. The colours were from memory, and the process of monotype allowed me to simplify the layers of water and mud, as well as capturing a sense of the landscape and the weather moving through."

Facing page: Conyer Curlew – Hugh Ribbans (linocut). Left: Curlew – Lisa Hooper (collagraph). Bottom, from left to right: Curlew (collagraph); Migration I (relief photopolymer); Migration VII (relief photopolymer) – all by Hester Cox. Page 52: Curlew and Cotton Grass – Hester Cox (collagraph).

Dipper

RUNNING UNDERWATER TO CATCH INVERTEBRATES;
nesting precariously under bridges, waterfalls and in riverside
walls; perching photogenically on slippery rocks – the Dipper
is well deserving of a place in this book. Not a bird many of us
will see often, or ever, it is neither plentiful nor easy to spot. It
is, however, a great subject for a print, as evidenced by Stuart
Brocklehurst's lovely linocut to the right, Lisa Hooper's etching
below and Louise Thompson's linocut overleaf.

Lisa explains that the River Almond near Cramond on the
Firth of Forth seemed an unlikely place to find a pair of Dippers
nesting. "The path is teeming with people, children and dogs in

Right: Sprite of the Beck – Stuart Brocklehurst (linocut).
Below: Dipper – Lisa Hooper (etching).

the summer and yet, there they were, undeterred. The water in this print has been treated rather playfully with concentric outlines and an overall variation in colour, forming a uniform yet interesting backdrop to the bird."

Stuart's Dipper print, entitled 'Sprite of the Beck', was made for an 'Up North Printmakers' group exhibition at Barrowford in the shadow of Pendle Hill. "Commonly seen on the river flowing alongside the mill housing the studios where the exhibition was held and on the streams of the nearby hillsides, it seemed an appropriate subject to represent the birdlife of the district."

Devon printmaker Louise Thompson encountered her Dipper at Watersmeet on Exmoor. She was unfamiliar with the species, looking it up on her return home. "They are lovely to watch perched on the stones on fast-flowing water. This is a reduction linocut. I love to keep the colours simple but have hopefully captured the movement of the water."

While the Dipper population has been relatively stable in most of the UK, water pollution in parts of Scotland, Wales, south-west and north-east England sadly means reduced numbers.

DIVERS

THE GREAT NORTHERN DIVER is the biggest of the UK species, on the Amber list and largely a winter visitor. Dining on fish and crustaceans, these birds are a spectacular sight thanks to their size and dramatic profile – often silhouetted against the sunlit sea.

Around 2,500 birds can over-winter in UK waters, making it something of a challenge for many would-be observers. Peter Brown is one who yearned for many years to see this bird. "However, life's fortunes turned and I began the first of many visits to the home of a friend in Canada, where I excitedly discovered 'loons' everywhere, even on the one-dollar coin (called a loonie)."

Above: Sheringham Shoal – Jeremy James (screenprint). Below: Rain Geese, Helga Water – Lisa Hooper (linocut).

Top: Great Northern Diver – Lisa Hooper (linocut). Above: Black-throated Diver, Assynt – Lisa Hooper (collagraph).

The Great Northern Diver in Peter's engraving on page 59 is in its winter plumage and visiting a small British harbour. Lisa Hooper's reduction linocut of the same species, to the left, was the result of a visit to Shetland. The bird is in full summer plumage. "A very lucky find. Its striking plumage and heavy bill make it a great subject for a printmaker."

According to Stuart Brocklehurst, "Great Northern Divers are a little bit special. Especially ones like the bird in my print [right] which turned up on a reservoir high on the moors one October still in immaculate full summer plumage."

In the startling print on page 59, Jeremy James contrasts the abstract plumage of the Diver with so-called 'Dazzle' camouflage used by warships. "Dazzle ships were used in both world wars – they had abstract patterns painted on their hulls in an attempt to confuse the enemy as to their heading, distance, etc. This appears to be 'confusing' a pair of Divers, maybe off Orkney."

Still harder to spot in the UK is the Black-throated Diver, with only 200 pairs breeding in the country and a winter population of fewer than 600 birds. Lisa Hooper's example, on page 56, was fishing in Clashnessie

Above: Great Northern Diver – Stuart Brocklehurst (linocut).

Bay, Assynt. "We watched for some time as it appeared and disappeared under the water and behind the spray.

"The wave in my resulting print is made by drizzling PVA glue on to the collagraph plate and manipulating it. It retains most of its form on drying and can be varnished to prevent it reactivating and sticking to the damp paper."

Lisa's reduction linocut entitled 'Rain Geese, Helga Water' on page 55 depicts the Red-throated Diver (also shown off the coast of north Norfolk on the same page by Jeremy James).

"While on Shetland for the first time recently, I was asked to produce some work for a gallery there," says Lisa. "This is one of a series of pieces inspired by that trip which was partly focused on looking for Red-throated Divers (also known as Rain Geese in northern Scotland where their cries are supposed to predict rain). Helga Water is in Northmavine on the north mainland."

Lisa's hand-coloured etching opposite was inspired by two Red-throated Divers in Clachtoll Bay, Assynt. "We had gone to Sutherland in search of Black-throated Divers but we were lucky enough to see a few Red-throated, too. I wanted to make a print that captured the watery and rather serene quality of the bay in the early morning light, and at the same time I wanted to preserve the loose sketch that I'd done from memory on my return. This proved to be quite a challenge, as drawing on to a zinc plate feels very different to drawing on paper, with both a slippery quality and also a tendency for the needle to stick every now and then. I use oil-based crayons for the aquatint resist, which gives a soft quality to the edges consistent with water."

DUNLIN

ACCORDING TO JACKIE CURTIS, STEART MARSHES IN SOMERSET IS A GREAT PLACE to find Dunlin. "The combination of a high tide with dawn light results in some lovely murmurations; as the Dunlin flock twists and flips, the light underside of one group contrasts with the dark backs of another group." The Dunlin is a relatively common small wader, with more than 9,500 breeding pairs in the UK and some 350,000 over-wintering in Britain. Spectacular flocks, sometimes in excess of 1,000 birds, can be seen on saltmarsh and grazing fields, resulting in scenes such as that depicted below by Jackie. Greta Hansen's reduction linocut opposite shows rather fewer birds on her patch of coastal Suffolk.

Left: Dunlin – Greta Hansen (linocut).
Below: Dunlin – Jackie Curtis (monoprint).

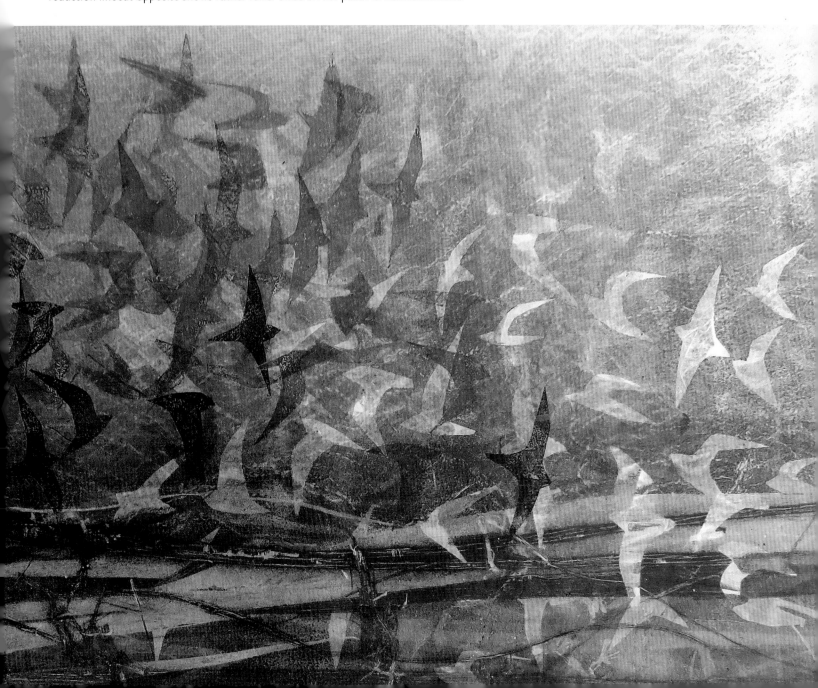

EGRET

Right: Little Egret – Richard Allen (linocut). Below: Little Egret – Kerry Buck (collagraph). Facing page, far right: Wolverstone Foreshore – Greta Hansen (woodcut). Facing page, left: Egret – Anne Townshend (linocut).

NOT SO MANY YEARS AGO, BIRDWATCHERS AND ARTISTS WOULD have had to travel to more exotic climes in order to spot Egrets in action. Nowadays, almost every British wetland environment boasts these startling white herons, usually the breeding Little Egret but occasionally a visiting Great Egret or Cattle Egret. Greta Hansen's woodcut print on the right, 'Wolverstone Foreshore', captures a Little Egret on the River Orwell in Suffolk, not far from the Royal Harwich Yacht Club.

Anne Townshend was amazed to see a large flock of them roosting in a small tree on Fingringhoe Reserve in Essex, resulting in the linocut print below. "The Little Egret has become a common sight in recent years, and I love its graceful flight, elegant shape, but slightly shaggy feathers."

The Little Egret was first seen in numbers on British soil during 1989; and first bred, in Dorset, in 1996. This range expansion from western and northern France has made it a common sight in the south of England,

Above: Egret Fishing – Nick Wonham (linocut). Left and far left: Ebb Tide and Saltmarsh – Valerie Sims (woodcut). Right: Watcher in the Willow – Jackie Curtis (linocut). Far right: Gone Fishing – Hugh Ribbans (linocut).

with more than 700 breeding pairs and 4,000-5,000 over-wintering birds.

The linocut print below entitled 'Watcher in the Willow' is by Jackie Curtis. "Over several months I observed, sketched and photographed this gnarled pollard willow stump in a rhyne on the Somerset Levels near us – a route marker for Egret, Buzzard, Kestrel and Heron which I saw perched on or beside the tree. The patterns of the Buzzard's feathers had similarities with that of the bark, so that the Buzzard extends from the tree in contrast to the smoother white Little Egret standing in the foreground."

Nick Wonham's reduction linocut opposite, 'Egret Fishing', is based on a bird seen at Suffolk's Minsmere reserve. The multi-block linocut on the right by Hugh Ribbans explores a similar theme on the north Kent marshes near his home. Richard Allen's linocut and Kerry Buck's collagraph on page 62 capture the typical Egret profile, while 'Ebb Tide' and 'Saltmarsh' by Valerie Sims opposite use north Norfolk as the backdrop for the birds.

EIDER

HOPEFULLY NOT SUFFERING FROM BODY IMAGE issues, the Eider is Britain's heaviest duck, but also the fastest in flight, suggesting that there is plenty of muscle under those pillow-bound feathers. A hearty appetite for molluscs means there is ongoing conflict between these birds and mussel farmers, who watch the large groups of highly gregarious birds riding the swell close inshore. The drakes are very handsome until they shed their breeding plumage and turn almost black. Their popularity with printmakers is obvious from this fine selection of work.

The complex linocut print on the right is all the more remarkable in that Yorkshire artist Mike Smith has been dealing with severe medical issues, and we are very pleased to be able to include this new work, based on Eiders seen off the Northumberland coast near the Farne Islands.

"Commissioned to undertake this print, I deliberately chose to make the soft, subtle textures of the female the focus of the work, rather than the more flamboyant, somewhat 'comical', plumage of the male."

Below we reproduce a triptych of three woodcut/

Right: Eider Ducks – Mike Smith (linocut).
Facing page: Nesting Eider – Kittie Jones (monotype).
Below: Eiders in Convoy: triptych (Full Ahead, Under Way, Drop Anchor) – Thelma Sykes (woodcut & linocut).

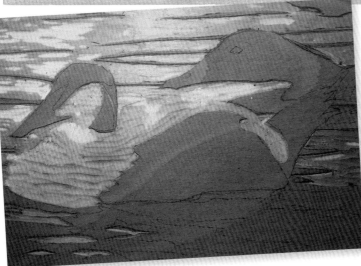

linocut prints by Thelma Sykes that has long graced a spot on our wall above the front door. The three self-contained prints are named 'Full Ahead', 'Under Way' and 'Drop Anchor'. They combine woodcut on red pine with six lino blocks, three of which were reduced progressively using the reduction method.

"I'm in Sutherland, ebb-tide, kelp fronds folding and bobbing parabolas above the swell: their curves find echoes in the arc of the Shag diving, the wing patches of a Tystie [black guillemot] – and in the plumage of the Eider drakes. Sturdy as barges, Eiders are round with plumage that exaggerates their form. Kelp fronds mirror

Top: Eiders, Cumbrae – Lisa Hooper (woodcut). Left: wood block for Eiders, Cumbrae. Above: Ardbeg – Jeremy James (linocut). Facing page, left: Land and Sea – Chris Sinden (linocut). Facing page, top: Eider Ducks – Sue Brown (collagraph). Facing page, bottom: Eider Down – Mary Collett (linocut).

the curves of the Eiders afloat alongside.

"I choose a plank of red pine to describe the sea loch, for its grain resembles moving water; but this grain both informs and constricts my composition, for each duck must create the wake behind it yet the ripples are dictated by the wood. My grain is open, with wake-like ripples, then narrows to a close, parallel grain – and this monotonous wood I remove completely. It gives a change of pace through my composition

from Eiders alert, in low-key display through to relaxed and settling in calm waters.

"My composition faltered for a year until, back in Sutherland, I saw a youngster in a stage of moult I'd not seen before: partly white on breast and back and with a hint, on the head, of those soft teardrop markings to come. He made all the difference, and the triptych came together.

"Work on cutting and proofing three wood blocks and six lino blocks begins. Printing the

triptych is a physical engagement with inks, rollers, paper, press – and fatigue. Gratefully, in my mind, I re-play Eiders cooing as I work, and it makes me smile."

The nesting Eider on page 67 is a monotype by Kittie Jones, created using this 'painterly' approach that yields just the one version, rather than an edition. "A nesting Eider is the perfect subject for an artist as she is very unlikely to move off her nest,

prioritising the protection of her eggs over her own safety. The one depicted in this print sat beautifully for me during a drawing trip to the Isle of May, and I was pleased to be able to translate my sketchbook drawing into a monotype, incorporating a sense of the island landscape beyond. In this print I used the process of working on a ghost print to be expressive in my mark-making and use of colour."

Lisa Hooper on page 68 provides a reduction woodcut entitled 'Eiders, Cumbrae', that is accompanied by a section of her original block. "I have experimented with different kinds of wood. As I quite like the grain to show, I started off with a relatively hard, grainy floor ply that I still use. It is rather hard on the tools and hands, and the grain can be intrusive. This print was made on a piece of hardwood ply that had quite a smooth finish but was nevertheless quite hard. The inks behave in the same way as they do on lino. These birds were off the coast of Great Cumbrae, an island in the Firth of Clyde."

The new 31-block linocut print on page 69 by Chris Sinden is named 'Land

and Sea'. "Two walking Slimbridge Eider become three. The birds were observed during a family break with the grandchildren." Chris has set them against a background of rocks from Bracelet Bay on the Gower Peninsula.

We apologise for not doing justice to the epic Eider linocut by Mary Collett on page 69, but nowhere in this book could we have captured the scale of her print – the biggest the artist has ever attempted. "It was carved from two pieces of A1-size lino – one for the background and one for the bird itself. The carving took forever, and I vowed never to attempt anything else quite as big! The printing was also tricky, placing such large pieces of paper over the lino and getting the registration correct."

Cambridgeshire artist Nina Sage contributed the linocut 'Eiders Wing North' on the facing page. "On a recent winter voyage up Norway's coast I felt I had really arrived in the Arctic Circle when I saw my first Eiders. The combination of the setting sun on the icy water, the birds as a focal point with a backdrop of magnificent snow-covered peaks, provided all the inspiration I needed to create the print."

Janice Earley concentrates above on the breeding plumage of the drakes at their most striking, contrasting well with the reflective water. Sue Brown's collagraph on page 69 also features the well-dressed males.

The small print opposite is a very early work by Robert Gillmor. 'Drake Eiders' from 1961 is a reduction linocut, based on birds seen at the Slimbridge reserve. Jeremy James, meanwhile, focuses on the female for his Ardbeg Distillery linocut on page 68.

Facing page, top: Eiders Wing North – Nina Sage (linocut). Facing page, bottom: Drake Eiders – Robert Gillmor (linocut). Above: Eiders – Janice Earley (linocut).

GANNET

THE SPECTACULAR GANNET IS MORE OFTEN DEPICTED IN action than at rest. Powerful in the air and under the water, the cigar shape and narrow wings are a dead giveaway for this species that occupies more than 200,000 nests in the UK.

Jane Smith captures the vertical dive into the sea and the pursuit

Far left: Cliffs at North Bay, Flamborough – Mike Smith (linocut). Left: Diving Gannets – Jane Smith (screenprint).
Above: Bempton Gannets – Jeremy James (linocut).

of fish below the surface in her prints on pages 72 and 75. "The Gannets took me by surprise. I knew they nested in the Shetland Islands, but I had gone there with scientists from the RSPB to study Puffins. Every day we walked across the peatlands on Unst, through the Skua colony, past displaying Dunlin and Snipe, to the sea-cliffs. One day I turned left to go exploring. And after a mile or so, I came upon Gannets, thousands of them, nesting right up to the top of the cliffs. When I returned home

I had field sketches to turn into screenprints in my studio. Usually I only draw what I have seen with my own eyes, but when I watched underwater footage of Gannets hunting fish, I wanted to celebrate their extraordinary abilities both above and below the surface."

Mike Smith's reduction linocut on page 77 was inspired by the RSPB reserve at Bempton Cliffs. "A bitterly cold day in early January with a ferocious easterly wind blowing in from the sea. On the plus side the

conditions resulted in a sparkling light, a sea of crystal blues and superb soaring conditions for the gannets!"

Another of Mike's prints, 'Cliffs at North Bay, Flamborough', represents the same stretch of Yorkshire coastline that provides the RSPB with the Bempton reserve. Jeremy James uses the location for his 'Bempton Gannets' on page 73, while the same artist produced the linocut 'Circling Gannets' on page 76 that shows the birds circling above a late summer

Page 74: Granite, Gannet, Annet – Carry Akroyd (serigraph). Page 75, clockwise from top left: Displaying Gannets – Jane Smith (screenprint); Gannets – Anne Townshend (linocut); Underwater Gannets – Jane Smith (screenprint); Gannet sketch by Jane Smith. Left: Circling Gannets – Jeremy James (linocut). Above: Jura – Jeremy James (linocut). Top right: Gannets from Bempton Cliffs – Mike Smith (linocut). Right: Gannet – Peter Brown (wood engraving).

Orkney harvest. 'Jura', the linocut above, is another of Jeremy's Gannet observations.

'Granite, Gannet, Annet' is a 2014 serigraph print by Carry Akroyd, reproduced on page 74. "I made the drawings for this sitting on rocks at the tip of St Agnes, Isles of Scilly, looking towards the island of Annet. The title came to me when Gannets flew close by."

Peter Brown's wood engraving on the right was inspired by childhood day trips to the Skellig islands, eight miles off the south-west tip of Ireland. "Small Skellig was passed close by on the outward and return journeys. It could not be landed on, and was home during the breeding season to 20,000 pairs of Gannets. This sight and smell was accompanied by a cacophony of bird calls and cries and the constant activity of gliding, soaring, diving and flapping wings."

GARGANEY

A SPECIES OF DUCK SOMEWHAT BIGGER THAN THE MORE familiar Teal, the male sports a dazzling white streak from above the eye to the base of the head. These are relatively shy birds, less numerous than Teal and inclined to lurk among the reeds rather than cruising open water. They leave the UK during August and September and head for Africa, returning between late February and April.

Robert Greenhalf's woodcut opposite was inspired by Continental birds rather than by British summer visitors. "Garganey always seem to be less skulking and easier to see on the other side of the Channel, so this print used as reference sketches made in the Baie de Somme area of France."

Peter Brown's wood engraving was made after a day spent visiting some gravel pits – "a day watching in hope for Kingfishers and searching the reeds for rare warblers, neither of which were seen. But in a sunny spot away from the swoosh of the distant bypass and the clucking of Coots, I sat and silently watched a young pair of Garganey ducks busying themselves in a small inlet. Their quiet occupation provided a much needed calm away from the urban stir."

Opposite: Garganeys – Robert Greenhalf (woodcut).
Left: Garganey – Peter Brown (wood engraving).

GODWIT

BRITAIN'S GODWIT COME IN TWO FLAVOURS, Black-tailed and Bar-tailed. The long-legged former is perhaps the more striking, with the male tending towards brick red summer plumage and the female largely grey in colouration. John Tennant's print on page 6 highlights the red of the male, while Anne Townshend (below) focuses on grey.

"This was the first reduction linoprint I ever attempted. It involves using just one block of lino,

cutting out one colour at a time, then printing, then cutting out the next colour and so on, until you are left with just a very fragile, skinny piece of carved lino for the final colour."

Mike Webb explains that Brent Geese feeding on a south coast estuary were the inspiration for his 'Godwit and Geese' linocut on the right. "I watched the geese on a slightly breezy October afternoon, when they had recently arrived for the winter. They were busy probing the mud, tugging at their favourite eelgrass, then wandering off to follow the receding tide. I had planned a linocut with just the geese, but they were surrounded by many waders and also ducks such as Wigeon, Shelduck and Teal. Nearest to the geese was a lovely flock of Black-tailed Godwit, and with all the activity of feeding and flying, one of these was included in my final design."

Max Angus entitled her linocut print 'The Jovial Breeze Sends Us Out to Play' (below right) after the Charles Kingsley poem 'Ode to the North East Wind'. "A sharp, cold wind from the North-East. The lazy wind that, instead of going around you, blows right through you. It's the breeze that takes away your breath and quickens your pace up the steepest of hills. The Godwit dare each other to fly the breeze as close as possible to the sea. From the hills overlooking the sea the swell of the sea seems to absorb the sky and land with its rise and fall."

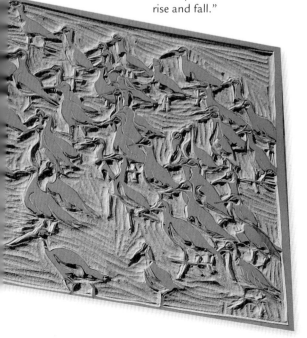

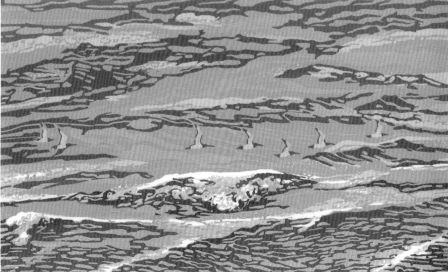

Shelduck and Godwit – Robert Greenhalf (woodcut).

GOLDENEYE

BOTH MALE AND FEMALE OF THIS DIVING DUCK SPECIES are distinctive, which allows greater gender equality as an artistic subject, and means that both are well represented in this combined woodcut and linocut print by Thelma Sykes. Breeding on wooded lakes and ponds, with nests in tree holes, these birds feed mainly on molluscs, crustaceans and insect larvae. Amber-listed in the UK, there are some 200 breeding pairs and up to 27,000 over-wintering birds. They first nested in Scotland in 1970, and adapt well to manmade nest boxes mounted on trees close to water.

"The grain on a plank of red pine prompted this print! As a tree matures, early-growth rings are compressed and the grain, widely spaced beneath the bark, narrows in the heartwood. Seen one way, the plank is wood-grain, but turn it and it takes on the perspective of rippled water. The cutting of the plank had also left vertical bite marks that suggested shimmer.

"Drake Goldeneye make fine linocut subjects. I love the stark plumage pattern and the hinted sheen of colour on their heads. After I inked the block for the darkest colour, I dabbed off ink where the heads would catch the light – a monoprint technique that let this colour gleam through.

"The Goldeneye were cut from lino blocks, and lining up the reflections with the wood grain was one problem to be solved. This detail [left] is from a proof to check that wood block and master lino block are in register. See the bit of lino left behind the head and above the back of the third bird from left at this stage; it will show me where to cut the wood block and the background lino block, and then it will be cut from this block before the editioning begins."

Overtures and Undercurrents – Thelma Sykes (woodcut/linocut).

GREBE

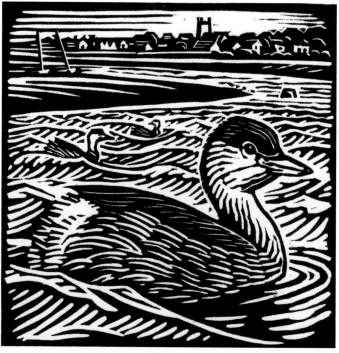

HERE ON THE BROADS, THE AUTHOR HAS A particular fondness for two types of British grebe. The Great Crested is perhaps the poster bird for the Norfolk Broads, seen almost everywhere on the network of rivers and shallow lakes. Mingling with Greylag Geese, Mute Swans and the various mongrel

Right: Little Grebe – Richard Allen (linocut). Below: A Moment of Reflection – Thelma Sykes (linocut). Opposite: Great Crested Grebes – Kerry Buck (collagraph).

Left: Bogbean – Thelma Sykes (woodcut). Below left: Black-necked Grebe sketches by Thelma Sykes. Facing page: Let's Dance – Lisa Hooper (linocut).

Bogbean plan taller than black grebe

ducks, the grebes ignore the offer of chips and sandwiches to compete with anglers for freshwater fish. Dabchicks, known correctly as Little Grebe, are another familiar sight at the river edges, emerging from the reeds to dive for invertebrates and small fish.

The Great Crested Grebes opposite were spotted by Lisa Hooper on the Sharpness Canal. This linocut print shows "quite a stylised approach to water. The printed ink has been applied in a blend, and the painting is also varied across the piece."

Norfolk collagraph artist Kerry Buck captures one of her Great Crested Grebe underwater (page 85), trailing air bubbles as it chases prey. Those of Thelma Sykes on page 84 were sketched in different places at different times, but became combined when the linocut was created. "I chose drawings of resting birds; the only action in the print would be a disturbance in the water just moving the birds' reflections as the storm began. One grebe I drew at Loch of Kinnordy, while the other was one of a pair at Grafham Water, Cambridgeshire."

Thelma also produced the woodcut above of the secretive Black-necked Grebe and young (only around 50 pairs breed in the UK). "I need patience to see them here at Loch of Kinnordy, where Bogbean plants form floating islands linked by hidden waterways. I hope the woodcut will convey something of the

Above left: Still Waters – Vanna Bartlett (linocut). Above right: Nesting Grebe – Vanna Bartlett (linocut). Left: Grebes – Jeremy James (linocut).

mystery of these grebes. Here, the flowering spikes of Bogbean dwarf the grebes, but I've shown only their disturbed reflections; there's a hint of the striped-humbug head of a young bird riding on the parent's back while a second circle of ripples suggests that its mate has just dived, collecting food for the young."

'Still Waters' (above left) is a study of Great Crested Grebes compiled from sketches that Vanna Bartlett made when cycling around Holland. "I loved sketching the family parties with the little stripey-headed youngsters riding on their parents' backs. This was one of my earliest linocuts and was printed simply as a single black block and then hand coloured with watercolour."

GULLS

Below: Bristol Blue Gull – Mary Collett (linocut). Top right: Lesser Black-backed Gull – Peter Brown (wood engraving). Bottom right: Beachcomber – Anne Townshend (linocut).

Far left: High and Dry – Rob Barnes (linocut). Above: Travelling Light, Little gulls and Sandwich Tern – Thelma Sykes (linocut). Left: Black-headed Gulls – Richard Allen (linocut).

Above left: Crosby Beach, Liverpool Bay – Mike Smith (linocut). Top right: Tyne Bridges – Mike Smith (linocut).
Above right: Beach Boys – Valerie Sims (woodcut). Facing page: Gulls at Woolacombe – Louise Thompson (linocut).

WITH GULLS, THERE IS ALWAYS THE RISK of the generic creeping into art. However, they are undeniably useful as a background feature or as an enhancement to a seaside image. Indeed, these pages are a mixture of the species-specific and the 'general gull'. They are a very versatile, prolific and often unloved group of birds, getting bad press for ice-cream and chip theft, poor toilet training and uncontrollable volume. These are, however, very smart birds – in all senses.

Ann Townshend's 'Beachcomber' linocut on page 89 was inspired by a large Herring Gull resident in Dorset. "She was named 'Darlin' by the couple who fed her and enjoyed her company on their decking overlooking the Heritage coastline. She would sit on the rail, close enough to touch, slightly disconcerting with her huge beak and her head cocked, beady eye focused on me as I sketched. It amused me carving this lino to put a live fossil in her beak (a very lucky find) for a scruffy beachcomber such as her."

On the far left, Mike Smith chooses Crosby Beach on the Merseyside coastline for his atmospheric linocut. "Situated immediately to the north of Liverpool Docks begin broad beaches that continue for nearly 20 miles to Southport and beyond. The first part, Crosby Beach, is home to Antony Gormley's sculpture 'Field'. As evening sets in, using a colour palette that must owe something to the industry of Merseyside, great flocks of gulls and waders appear, to then settle in anticipation of approaching night."

Mike Webb has taken a far more detailed

approach to his gull linocut, above. "Great Black-backed Gulls tend to form small parties rather than large flocks, and I had seen them far out on an exposed sandbar, where other gulls roost at low tide. The two adults and a few first-winter birds were very noticeable, due to their size and impressive plumage, against a backdrop of pastel yellow-ochre sand. They preened and slept in the warm autumn sun, the receding tide to their advantage. I enjoyed cutting out the bold markings on the birds for my linocut, and the contrast between the

adult and younger gull became the main focus for my design."

Thelma Sykes has chosen a far less common species of gull for her linocut 'Travelling Light' on page 91. "You cannot visit Minsmere in September and fail to be moved by the colour. The heaths lose their brashness as heather begins to seed into subdued purple-browns and bronze. It had been a dry summer; water levels were low. The water carried so much mud in suspension that it became opaque and echoed the

browns of the heath. I needed to record these unexpected colours and saw them echoed in the plumage of the Little Gulls that were gathering alongside a Sandwich Tern, just a drop-in on their travels.

"*Larus minutus*! Tiny they are, yet hugely charismatic. These youngsters fledged this summer in the marshes of Siberia and are heading south west to winter offshore as far as West Africa. But they like shallow water and muddy sandbanks, and as a stopover for a few days Minsmere is just perfect."

Peter Brown encountered his Lesser Black-backed Gulls (page 89) on a country walk through arable land. "There they were, a surprising sight: many gathered on freshly ploughed fields seemingly quite at home by a glade of oaks with crows, wood pigeons and hedgerow birds all around."

According to Louise Thompson, the gulls at the water's edge on Woolacombe Beach (page 93)

"create white shapes against the stripes of blue waves and wet sand. This is what I wanted to focus on – more of the impression of gulls against the sea rather than an accurate representation of the birds. I walk Woolacombe Beach a lot with my spaniel, and invariably he chases them and makes them fly – I wanted to capture some of that movement yet keep it simple with the colours."

Mary Collett's 'Bristol Blue Gull' that opens this section is based on a Herring Gull and the use of this particular shade of blue. Norfolk linocut artist Rob Barnes populates many of his landscape prints with birds, and here we reproduce two that use gulls to great effect, as foreground interest in 'Down to the Sea' (above), as well as spiralling over the Suffolk coastline in 'High and Dry' (page 90).

Facing page: Great Black-backed Gulls – Michael Webb (linocut). Above: Down to the Sea – Rob Barnes (linocut).

HARRIER

Left: Harrier at Melvich – Thelma Sykes (linocut).
Below: Parkgate Marsh sketch of Hen Harriers by
Thelma Sykes. Above: Marsh Harrier – Peter Brown
(wood engraving). Facing page: Hunting Harrier –
Robert Gillmor (linocut).

PARKGATE MARSH

SOME OF US HAVE BEEN LUCKY enough to see more than one type of harrier sailing majestically over coastal locations, as the highly persecuted Hen Harrier visits marshland habitats, while the Marsh Harrier has a stronghold in Norfolk both on the Broads and on the coast.

The Hen Harrier's unfortunate choice of moorland nesting sights has exposed it to the wrath of landowners seeking to protect game birds. The result is plummeting numbers, particularly in England. The birds can be seen on passage and during winter over coastal meadows, but are a much rarer sighting than their cousin the Marsh Harrier.

Not surprisingly, artists tend to capture Marsh Harriers flying low, back and forth, above reedbeds seeking prey. The diet varies from small mammals to frogs, birds and nestlings. Robert Gillmor's three-colour linocut to the right was created as the cover for a 2003 book *In the Countryside* that reproduced newspaper columns of the same name by writer Moss Taylor for the *Eastern Daily Press*. Robert chose a familiar corner of north Norfolk for the inspiration, being a resident of Cley-next-the-Sea, a birdwatchers' mecca. The 'Hunting Harrier' that gives the print its name will have been seeking prey rather bigger than the dragonfly seen here!

Peter Brown also portrays the magnificent predator on the prowl with his wood engraving on

page 96. "An early start for a cold day at a wetland reserve. So much was promised and so little seen. But, towards evening, far across the fens and the sea of gently swaying reeds, this distant figure appeared. On broad wings, with its head down watchful on what was below, the Marsh Harrier quartered the ground and gradually came closer. Half an hour later and a memorable day was complete. A happy glow of contentment and talk of our unbelievable luck and our harrier filled the pub that night."

Carry Akroyd's 2011 serigraph opposite is entitled 'Broadland Winter Afternoon' and shows the Marsh Harrier in an environment particularly familiar to the author, as it is only a couple of miles down the road. "I spent one of those short days of midwinter wandering around different sides of Hickling Broad, peering through reedbeds, standing on tiptoe on higher ground," says Carry. "Sunset came early, and the most astonishing redness reflected everywhere."

With Richard Allen's small linocut of the Marsh Harrier (opposite) that appears in his own *Coastal Birds* mini-book, we have included the artist's preliminary sketches. "Female and immature birds are largely dark brown with rich cream-coloured crowns, and patches on the forewing. Males are smaller and have black wingtips, pale grey panels in the wings, and a buffy-rufous body."

Rob Barnes, as a Norfolk resident, has greater regular access to the Marsh Harrier than many artists, with his wetlands raptor avoiding the unwelcome attention of crows in the linocut above.

Left: Marsh Harrier – Rob Barnes (linocut). Above right: Marsh Harrier sketches and linocut – Richard Allen. Right: Broadland Winter Afternoon – Carry Akroyd (serigraph).

Heron

Left: Heron – Andy English (wood engraving). Right: The Complete Angler – Stuart Brocklehurst (linocut). Below: Winter Heron – Chris Sinden (linocut). Facing page: Heron and Shelducks – Robert Greenhalf (woodcut).

AS EVIDENCED BY ANDREW HASLEN'S HAND-coloured linocut above, there can be drama when the Grey Heron is about, even though most artists choose to show these large and majestic birds either hunched or standing tall in a patient wait for prey.

Along with the Kingfisher, perhaps the archetypal bird of the waterways, the heron is far from rare but can still provide a thrill when it flaps slowly overhead or emerges silently from the reeds, dagger beak flashing as it strikes for a fish or frog.

Ely-based wood engraver Andy English shares this enthusiasm for the birds. "When we were first married we lived in a tiny, isolated hamlet in the Norfolk Fens. A little way along the road from us was a copse of trees that was a heronry. Watching the birds roost and nest up in the treetops was a sight – and sound – to remember. I have always had a liking for these birds. I love their patience as they stand waiting for food. They are a real favourite of mine, and I have engraved them more than any other bird."

Deborah Vass also based her heron print on page 105 on a Norfolk sighting, this time on her home patch of Diss. "A resident Grey Heron is a favourite, stalking at the Mere's edge and making a stab at unsuspecting fish."

Herons fascinate Somerset artist Jackie Curtis, who

Above: Heron Mobbed by Crows – Andrew Haslen (linocut). Far right: Herons – Jackie Curtis (woodcut). Right: sketch by Jackie Curtis for Herons woodcut. Bottom right: Heron, Hemshaw – Valerie Sims (woodcut).

*Above left: Harnser –
Robert Gillmor (linocut).
Above right: Dovedale
Heron – Andy English
(wood engraving). Left:
Heron Flying – Lisa Hooper
(woodcut). Facing page,
from top left clockwise:
Heron – Deborah Vass
(linocut); The Midnight Pool
– Ian MacCulloch (linocut);
Heron Chopa – Caroline
Barker (linocut).*

admires their "majestic" stature despite their ungainly flight. Her large woodblock on page 103 was cut from ash that left beautiful wood grain in the finished print. A preliminary sketch of the impressive print is also featured.

Found above Chris Sinden's 29-block

linocut of a chilly looking heron in winter on page 100 is Stuart Brocklehurst's 'Complete Angler' – a linocut print made specifically to be used as a cover illustration for the Huddersfield Birdwatchers Club annual report.

A particularly atmospheric linocut print

has been provided by Ian MacCulloch with 'The Midnight Pool' on page 105, where a Kingfisher casts an envious eye over the heron's lucky catch.

The heron in flight is a little ungainly, although the sheer size and the slow wingflaps always catch the attention. Caroline Barker on the left captures the stately progress, while Lisa Hooper's reduction woodcut on page 104 has a simple colour scheme and utilises the woodgrain for the water effect.

The blocks for Robert Gillmor's 'Harnser' (page 104) were cut while staying at York University during an RSPB annual members' weekend. "There was a small tree, covered in blossom, with narrow grey-green leaves, outside the exhibition hall where I sat each year, demonstrating watercolour painting or linocutting. Attracted by the tree's decorative possibilities, I went outside and drew the twigs directly on to the lino, returning inside to start cutting. The first of five blocks."

A brand-new heron linocut by Robert appears below, completed in the summer of 2018 and representing the artist's final linocut for that year, which was compromised by health issues.

Left: Heron on Gold – Caroline Barker (linocut).
Below left: Grey Heron – Richard Allen (linocut).
Below: Stalking Heron – Robert Gillmor (linocut).

KINGFISHER

A BOOK LIKE THIS COULD HARDLY OMIT THE Kingfisher, beloved by all but the small fish it preys on. We have taken the liberty of reproducing on the left a 1979 etching from our own collection of wildlife art, by the late David Koster and combining the brilliant birds with Yellow Flag Iris in bloom. Richard Allen's linocut from Coastal Birds appears below and the artist observes that "despite their bright colours, rich orange breast, blue-green crown and wings, with a gleaming cerulean blue back, they can be surprisingly hard to spot when perched in a quiet corner."

The sequence of four Kingfisher linocuts by Richard Jarvis on page 108 actually appear framed in line, but we rearranged them to suit our layout. "Rutland Water hides are fruitful, allowing excellent sketching opportunities for species such as Kingfishers and Snipe. I was able to watch a Kingfisher fishing from perches in front of Crake hide, resulting in my Kingfisher sequence print.

"For the majority of my prints I use oil-based ink, these are then hand-tinted with watercolour. Sketches may be traced directly from the sketchbook on to the lino for a print or, alternatively, the sketches are used as the inspiration for a design that is then transferred to the lino block."

It is surprising how well the Kingfisher can be portrayed when limited to black and white. As well as Richard Allen's

Left: Kingfishers – David Koster (etching - from author's collection). Below: Kingfisher – Richard Allen (linocut).

linocut, wood engraver Andy English captures the essence of the colourful bird in his print on the right. "It is always a pleasure to see a Kingfisher, even if it is only a glimpse of a blue streak beside the water. There is a tributary of the River Cam where I would see one regularly and, since I like to engrave a bird in a real setting, I engraved 'Kingfisher at Bourn Brook' with a favourite group of trees in the background."

Suffolk-based Andrew Haslen is something of a Kingfisher specialist, with his paintings and prints of the birds overshadowed only by his huge portfolio of hares. We combine here 'old' and 'new' styles of linocut printmaking, in that the image on page 109 is one of his most recent, produced using the multi-block process, while the prints on the left and right are from a period when Andrew tended to hand-colour his black-printed linocuts – these appearing in the book *Halcyon* that we produced for the artist a few years ago.

'Halcyon' is also the name of Vanna Bartlett's linocut print (top right). "It was sketched at the coast one winter when I was lucky to find one perched on a small boat. It was one

of those rare occasions when a picture presented itself in its entirety rather than having to sketch several elements and bring them together into a suitable composition

back in the studio. I loved the primary palette of the blue Kingfisher and the red paintwork on the prow of the boat. The grey ropes added a nice bit of texture."

Page 108: Kingfisher 1-4 – Richard Jarvis (linocut). Page 109: Kingfisher – Andrew Haslen (linocut). Opposite: Kingfisher at Sunset – Andrew Haslen (linocut). From top left, clockwise: Kingfisher at Bourn Brook – Andy English (wood engraving); Halcyon – Vanna Bartlett (linocut); Halcyon – Andrew Haslen (linocut).

K**ITTIWAKE**

2nd August 2010
Adult and Juvenile Kittiwake
Braidcarr Point, Seahouses.
2.00 pm - 10 minutes drawing before the rain started and the ink began to run.

Left: Brooding Kittiwake
– Robert Gillmor
(linocut). Above and right:
ink and watercolour
preliminary sketches by
Stuart Brocklehurst for
Kittiwakes (linocut)
on facing page, top.
Facing page, bottom:
Kittiwake – Peter Brown
(wood engraving).

SADLY, THE KITTIWAKE IS CAUSING increasing conservation concern, and bird lovers should seek every opportunity to watch these lovely birds during their breeding visits to rugged coastline and the occasional bridge and building.

Stuart Brocklehurst's print above was developed from field sketches drawn during a family holiday on the Northumberland coast. "I go for a walk with a sketchbook, make drawings of anything that interests me, then back in the studio use these drawings to make the best print that I can. I sketch predominantly with pen and ink. The positive irreversible nature of the mark forces me to really look and concentrate on the subject. If time and the subject allows, I may then make another coloured study in watercolour [see top left]. In the studio the composition is refined and the sequence of printing decided upon."

Peter Brown produced the wood engraving on the right. "The Kittiwake strikes me as a remarkably delicate bird to inhabit such a dangerous place. With its slender bill and fine features it seems too demure to mix it with the black-backs and the vertical cliffs where it chooses to roost and bring up its young. I admire this bird for its light elegance, its aerial skill and its fortitude."

Robert Gillmor's 'Brooding Kittiwake' is a linocut from 1967, inspired by a spring sojourn in Skomer.

Lapwing

WHEN PLANNING THIS BOOK, WE knew with absolute certainty that Avocet, Oystercatcher and this species would yield the biggest and most varied contribution. One of Robert Gillmor's 'walking linocuts', the Lapwing blends colour, shape, size and character to charm the most hide-hardened wildlife artist.

Robert, who contributes 'Peewit and Son' on the right, admits that "Lapwings have probably been the subject of more of my linocut prints than any other species. They are ideal, with a bold distribution of black and white plumage and that splendid crest. Of course, they are far from simply black and white, with greens and purple, terracotta and ochre revealed gloriously by bright sunlight.

"Their plaintive calls resulted in their old country name Peewit, which I was glad to use in the print of an adult and chick." These birds are also known as Green Plover, and another of Robert's linocuts with that name appears on page 119. John Hatton's linocut of the birds on page 116 also emphasises the green revealed in sunlight.

While particularly abundant near wetland habitats, Lapwings head farther inland to fields and meadows where they compete (often unsuccessfully) with gulls for worms. In flight, they are a wonderful spectacle thanks to the unique wing shape and their aerial acrobatics –

Right: Peewit and Son – Robert Gillmor (linocut). Facing page: Lapwings and Seabite – Robert Greenhalf (woodcut).

Facing page, far left: Reflective Mood – Thelma Sykes (woodcut/linocut).
Facing page, top right: Green Plover – John Hatton (linocut). Facing page,
below right: Trecheyre – David Hunt (etching). This page, top: Lapwing, close –
David Hunt (etching). Above: Bad Weather Blues – Thelma Sykes (linocut).
Right: Lapwing – Peter Brown (wood engraving).

Left: Lapwings – Richard Jarvis (linocut). Below left, Lapwing sketch by Richard Jarvis. Above: Lapwing Nest – Ian MacCulloch (linocut). Facing page: Green Plovers – Robert Gillmor (linocut).

see 'Counterpoint' by Thelma Sykes on page121. The same artist portrays them in a less joyful setting with her 'Bad Weather Blues' on page 117.

The sketch and linocut on the left are by Richard Jarvis. Much of his wildlife watching and sketching is concentrated around the many reservoirs in his local counties of Leicestershire, Rutland and Northamptonshire, resulting in subjects for several of his linoprints. "The print of Lapwings used drawings done at Eyebrook Reservoir, using my car as a hide with my scope set up on a car window mount, a good place to be on colder late autumn and winter days!"

Peter Brown, whose wood engraving appears on page 117, loves to see Lapwings. "Wherever I go, I take time to stop and notice again their shape, listen to their calls and delight in watching their fumbling flight. These characteristics make me smile, and I am reassured by their presence. I always think favourably

of a place where I have seen Lapwings."

The combination woodcut and linocut 'Reflective Mood' by Thelma Sykes on page 116 is based on field sketches made at different times and in places as far apart as Norfolk and Scotland. "In my mind these Lapwings are on the Dee, with the pale scalloping on the mantles of the young birds setting the time of year. Here I chose a rough piece of plywood and cut the block so that the grain runs top to bottom. Slivers of wood peel away when I open the grain with a wire brush and as I cut the reflections: it suggests the shimmer on watery muds when the block is printed, and it gives my Lapwing their resting place.

"This is a high-key work, with maximum contrast. It was to show a cold north light, almost austere; there are bright highlights, deep darks and few tonal steps from dark to light. In some lights the birds on my print look just black and white, at times there is a hint of green, and in some lights the birds really do appear to *be* green – but then that's Lapwing all over."

Facing page: Seashore Lapwings – Rob Barnes (linocut). Above left: Lapwing – Deborah Vass (linocut). Above right: Counterpoint – Thelma Sykes (linocut). Left: Lapwings – Richard Allen (linocut).

MERGANSER

Below: A Paddling of Mergansers – Lisa Hooper (collagraph).
Facing page: Winter Pond – Jeremy James (linocut).

WE ARE CHEATING A BIT HERE, BECAUSE we've combined *Mergus merganser* with *Mergus serrator*, both of which are sawbills. There are just two artist contributions for these large and striking diving ducks, pairing Lisa Hooper's Red-breasted Mergansers with the Goosanders of Jeremy James.

The Goosander first bred in Scotland in 1871: it remained a Northern resident until it began spreading throughout the UK in the 1970s – bringing it into conflict with anglers as the birds love a taste of trout or salmon. They appear below on Jeremy's snowbound pond, which presumably represents a short-term resting place as little suitable food is likely to exist. There are between 3,000 and 4,000

breeding pairs in the UK, but there can be 12,000 Goosander wintering in Britain – hence the pond visit below. "This is a pond I regularly cycle past," says Jeremy. "In winter, Goosander are regular visitors to this water: they are a very wary bird, staying to the centre of the pond. I always think they look slightly guilty, as though being caught somewhere where they shouldn't be."

Lisa's collagraph print opposite is 'A Paddling of Mergansers', which was inspired by a group fencountered on the shores of Loch Ryan.

"The medium of collagraph is very sensitive and produces an effect very much like an etching. It permits quite a strongly graphic

approach without having to work with the size restrictions imposed by an etching (typically, the zinc plate or the etching tray will determine the size of the latter in a home studio).

"The plate is made out of a cardboard mountboard with a paper surface. The aim is to introduce shallow textures that can hold ink in their depressions. I use acrylic medium and various tools to cut or dent the board as well as removing the paper surface of the board to reveal the filler (which holds more ink). The plate is varnished and surface wiped before being inked in several colours and printed under pressure on to damp paper (in one pass), like an etching. In most cases, hand colouring is required."

Moorhen

NESTING AMONG THE REEDS AT THE RIVER'S EDGE, AND WITH sooty black balls of down as young, the Moorhen is a popular bird, nowadays cohabiting village ponds with Mallard and various mongrel ducks. Caroline Barker encountered the subject for her linocut (right) on her local pond. "A W B Yeats quote came to mind: tread softly because you tread on my dreams."

Vanna Bartlett's linocut on the facing page, entitled 'Snowdrop Walk', was inspired by a chance encounter on a winter's day walk "when a Moorhen emerged from a dyke and delicately picked its way through a patch of snowdrops that were just thrusting up through the dead leaves and thin layer of snow. It looked so incongruous that I had to make it into a linocut."

The Deborah Vass linocut opposite features the nest, built like an island with sheltering vegetation of reeds, rushes, willow and other

similar material. The print on the left by Greta Hansen shows the young slightly beyond the 'fluffball' stage but still demanding their diet of largely plant matter being gathered by the parents.

Facing page: Family Group – Greta Hansen (linocut). Above: Tread Softly – Caroline Barker (linocut). Below: Tending the Nest – Deborah Vass (linocut). Right: Snowdrop Walk – Vanna Bartlett (linocut).

Osprey

WE HAD EXPECTED A FEW MORE waterside raptors to grace this collection, with the Osprey perhaps the next most obvious choice after the Marsh Harrier. Thankfully, Stuart Brocklehust delivered this fine eight-colour reduction linocut of the large, narrow-winged fish-eater that generally nests high in the pines following its return to the UK in April from West Africa.

"I live in the Calder Valley in the West Riding of Yorkshire, a predominantly upland area of moorland and steep-sided wooded valleys. Large open bodies of low-lying water suitable for breeding waterfowl are scarce. The area does, however, have a number of upland reservoirs which, while being of limited attraction to breeding birds, do in the right conditions turn up good records of passage waterfowl and waders.

"Another cover illustration for the Huddersfield Birdwatchers Club annual report, the prints created for the publication's format pose something of a challenge. Bleeding the wingtips of the Osprey out of the top and bottom of the shape was an attempt to add an extra element to this format. While the print is fine, the design didn't really work well with the accompanying text on the cover and it isn't a device that I have used since. This is one of those techniques, like having a dark border around the print, that when I see other printmakers doing it I really like. But when I try it on my own prints I'm never really happy with the result!"

OYSTERCATCHER

IT WILL COME AS NO GREAT surprise that the humble Oystercatcher is the most popular printmaking subject, going by the number and variety of interpretations submitted for inclusion – most of which are reproduced here. As with the Lapwing and Avocet, there is a great shape, size and colour scheme. These are by no means rare birds, but this doesn't diminish their appeal. They come with excellent sound effects; and their whirring flight, accompanied by persistent calling, means they are

Page 127: Oystercatchers – Robert Gillmor (linocut). Facing page, top: Oystercatchers at Cley – Nick Wonham (linocut). Facing page, bottom: Oystercatchers – Caroline Barker (linocut). Above: Oystercatchers, Evening – Robert Greenhalf (woodcut).

always memorable, on the hunt for molluscs, or for worms when away from the coast.

According to Robert Gillmor, the design for the 2000 linocut print on the opening page of this section was built up from a series of sketches of resting and preening birds. "They were drawn during one of my regular visits to Titchwell in north Norfolk. I would arrive early and create a tiny studio in a corner of a hide, clamping my telescope to the ledge below the narrow observation windows. It was fascinating to note the changes in lighting on the birds as the sun rose and moved around the wide Norfolk sky."

As with the artist's 'Sea Pies' on page 137, this is an example of the elimination print – a technique used infrequently by Robert, who generally favours multi-block linocuts where each colour is applied to a separate block. "I 'cheated' by using a second block for the bright orange-red bill and eyes. If I had not done so, it would have meant printing one of the blues over the orange-red, and this could have given me unwelcome problems. All the other colours were in a tight range of blues, from very light to very dark, with black used as the penultimate colour.

"The composition of 'Sea Pies', a group of Oystercatchers resting and preening, was developed from the sketches of just one or two birds as they stood and preened, watched through a small telescope clamped to the hide shelf, leaving my hands free to draw. I prefer an angled eyepiece, rather than straight, as it is easier to look through and sketch at the same time."

Caroline Barker, responsible for the 'Lannacombe Oystercatchers' above, sees them often "poking about on the mud in the estuary and flitting along the beaches". Norfolk printmaker Rob Barnes uses the birds regularly in his colourful East Anglian-themed linocut landscapes such as 'Riverside Walk' seen opposite.

Anne Townshend has made use of the strong monochrome aspects of the bird for her black-and-white linocut on page 135. "My favourite wader is the sturdy Oystercatcher, all black and white with strong, straight orange bill. It's lovely to hear its piping call over the water. I had been intending to make a simple black-and-white print for some while. Once completed, I so enjoyed working in traditional monochrome that I searched photos and books for other birds with striking black-and-white plumage to carve and print a series."

Max Angus, known best for her subtle hues and bird-adorned landscape prints, turned to a different medium and a different colour palette for 'Morston I' on page 134.

Facing page: Riverside Walk – Rob Barnes (linocut). Above: Lannacombe Oystercatchers – Caroline Barker (linocut).

"Taking sketches from Morston on the coastal path in the direction of Blakeney. Within 30 yards there were small boats, a quay, a church, trees, hedges, Oystercatchers

Facing page, top: High Tide – Robert Greenhalf (woodcut). Facing page, far left: Seapies and the Retreating Tide – Max Angus (linocut). Facing page, right: Resting with Oystercatchers – Max Angus (linocut). This page, top left: Oystercatcher – Richard Allen (linocut). Bottom left: Oystercatchers at Lee Bay – Louise Thompson (linocut). Above right: Breakfast for Oystercatchers – Rob Barnes (linocut).

Left: Two Oystercatchers – Fiona Carver (linocut).
Above: Morston I – Max Angus (wood engraving).
Facing page, from top left clockwise: Lighthouse
Peepers – Vanna Bartlett (linocut); Oystercatchers
on the Deben – Greta Hansen (linocut);
Oystercatchers – Anne Townshend (linocut).

and muddy creeks. I wanted to try and keep some of the integrity of the sketches in the mark-making. The wood block was only 7.5cm x 10cm. It was a lot to fit in to such a challenging size.

"Recently I had the opportunity to revisit wood engraving. I had not created any artwork so small for 20 years. Initially, I was intrigued to apply my knowledge of linocutting to the medium of wood engraving. Wood engraving captures such small details. How differently could a linocut printmaker create a wood engraving image?"

Richard Allen's black-and-white linocut on page 133 is the last of the monochrome contributions, another from his *Coastal Birds* series. "Feeding on shellfish, they use their strong bills to smash into or prise open cockles and mussels."

Fiona Carver's 'Two Oystercatchers' above is a five-block linocut depicting her favourite water bird. "Here they are standing on the cliff-edge, looking out to sea, a familiar sight in the spring when they are starting to nest.

"The subtle colour palette directs the viewer's attention to the birds, their legs and beaks standing out against the grey sea and sky. I sketched the birds on the cliffs in Anglesey before heading into the studio to work on the composition of the print. I carved five blocks, one for each colour, before inking them up and printing them in layers to produce the final image."

Greta Hansen's birds, seen on the far right, were spotted on the River Deben near Woodbridge in Suffolk, shortly afterwards becoming this reduction linocut.

'Feeding Oystercatchers' is a monotype by Kittie Jones on page 136. "A print made soon after a day spent sketching on the beach at Musselburgh, watching hundreds of Oystercatchers busily probing for food and squabbling over their finds.

"All the birds were feeding energetically, rummaging in the mud and pools with their beaks, emerging with dark, round shellfish and running low to the ground to somewhere they could enjoy them undisturbed. In the monotype I was aiming to give a sense of the expansive quality of the mudflat and the cool, winter light while

also being playful with layering and mark-making."

Jeremy James celebrates Scotland's whisky distilleries in a series of linocut prints, and 'Laphroaig', on the Isle of Islay, also boasts a pair of Oystercatchers (page 140).

The highly atmospheric woodcut by Robert Greenhalf on page 129 is, according to the artist, "more about light than about Oystercatchers!" However, the birds share a starring role in the same artist's 'High Tide' on page 132.

Max Angus returns to the world of colour for a second Oystercatcher-themed print. 'Resting with Oystercatchers' on page 132 sits alongside a new

linocut entitled 'Seapies and the Retreating Tide', making use of one of the many archaic names for the bird, shared with Robert Gillmor's image opposite.

Max writes about "Hunstanton on a cool, bright day in June. Rock-pooling can be a fascinating pastime. On this day, the tide had seemed to have left nothing but winkles and the tiniest barnacled mussels in the rockpools. The Oystercatchers [in 'Resting with Oystercatchers'] were preoccupied just standing there with nothing better to do than watch the tourists and their bewildering activities on the beach."

The woodcut print overleaf by Nina Sage, 'Along

Facing page: Sea Pies – Robert Gillmor (linocut). Above: Feeding Oystercatchers – Kittie Jones (monotype).

the Coast', depicts Oystercatchers near LLigwy beach on Anglesey, "an island I have been visiting for many years and have come to know well. The distinctive call of the Oystercatchers and their striking plumage are evocative of my visits there, and I have spent many a happy hour observing them while enjoying the peace of the island's glorious beaches."

'Lighthouse Peepers' on page 135 by Vanna Bartlett came about after a trip to Orford Ness in Suffolk. "The lighthouse standing lone sentinel against the sea on the shifting shingle was an irresistible subject. A small flock of Oystercatchers farther along the beach was a perfect addition to the composition, but I reduced their number to three in homage to the number of keepers who would have once manned the light – so it became Lighthouse Peepers (a name we use for Oystercatchers after their loud 'peeping' calls) rather than Keepers.

Oystercatchers are a favourite bird of Louise Thompson (page 133). "I love spotting them feeding on the rocks at Lee Bay. The challenge with creating a reduction linocut print of these birds was to keep the image simple yet get a splash of orange for their beaks and legs. I wanted to show the environment they exist in with the grey rocks and incoming tide."

Hugh Ribbans in his 'Conyer

Oystercatcher' above returns to the winding creeks of his north Kent home. "Walking to the window with cup of tea in hand, one is often treated to a fishing and diving performance from such visitors as Curlews, Oystercatchers, Mallards, Grebes and Little Egrets, all working their way up the creek feeding in the mud at low tide.

"It is little wonder that when I sit at my table roughing out ideas for new linocut prints, water birds, boats and mud naturally spring to mind.

"Most of my prints are linocuts, and I enjoy working out a multi-block print with separate colours and a key block. Not for me the 'sudden death' of the reduction process!"

Facing page: Along the Coast – Nina Sage (woodcut).
Above: Conyer Oystercatcher – Hugh Ribbans (linocut).

Above: Laphroaig – Jeremy James (linocut).

PHALAROPE

A RATHER RARE, AND SADLY DECLINING, BREEDER IN Scotland, where male numbers barely exceed 20, the tiny Red-necked Phalarope has the eye-catching habit of spinning around on the water to disturb plankton and mosquito larvae which it then consumes with great enthusiasm.

These birds winter at sea in the Indian Ocean, returning in late April to early June. Perhaps 30 more birds visit the UK during passage. Grey Phalarope do not breed in Britain.

Lisa Hooper has observed the species, resulting in the

linocut print 'Red-necked Phalarope' that opens this section.

"We set out in search of these little birds on Shetland. A small number of them come to Fetlar (reached from mainland Shetland via Yell and Unst) in the summer, to the Mire of Funzie. If you are lucky you will virtually stumble across them at your feet by the lochside. This hand-coloured linocut captures the movement in the water and the bright colours of the little bird."

'Funzie Phalaropes' above uses a different method. "This print is made from three cardboard plates that have been carved out like lino. The shallowness leads to random effects with ink layers in cutaway areas showing through. The design is deliberately bold to accommodate this."

Page 141: Red-necked Phalarope – Lisa Hooper (linocut). Above: Funzie Phalaropes – Lisa Hooper (mixed media).

P INTAIL

Above: Sundown – Thelma Sykes (linocut).

THIS HANDSOME SPECIES OF DUCK visits in large numbers during the winter, with approaching 30,000 birds occupying the Dee and Solway Estuaries, the Ouse Washes and other sheltered coastal habitats. They do breed in the UK, but in very small numbers; and, unfortunately, can be shot during the winter under our confused and archaic rules.

Thelma Sykes focuses her attention on the drakes with her four-colour linocut, left, made in 1998. "This day at WWT Martin Mere was a washout. Everything, everyone, was wet, dark, grey; the hide emptied, visitors left early to squelch to their cars. Then, in the last half-hour of daylight, the sky cleared to rain-washed blue, and a hint of sun from below the horizon suffused the duck in unexpected colour.

"A couple of scrappy sketches of Pintail drakes grabbed then gave me this composition, realised in black and white and published as a cover for *British Birds*. Yet the colour haunted me, and 18 months later I settled to cutting the two

Above: Pintail – Jeremy James (linocut). Left: All the Realms of Nature Mine – Max Angus (linocut).

blocks that became 'Sundown'. There are just four colours that overprint and blend: the blue and red of the first two printings are obvious, but it required a surprisingly vivid turquoise in the third printing and a deep purple in the last to describe that strangely luminous light."

No expense was spared by Jeremy James for the hand-coloured linocut above. A crescent moon applied in gold leaf provides the nocturnal setting for this drake. "Pintails are possibly my favourite duck: wonderful markings and a distinctive long and elegant tail."

Another poetic title by Max Angus for her Pintail print on the left, and it is nice to see ducks as well as drakes here – although the former are clearly busy looking for food.

"Lots of elegant Pintails at Cley [Norfolk] on a spring afternoon. Then they all turn upside down with their bottoms in the air. These delightful migrating ducks take advantage of these large expanses of pools at Cley. Nature may have bred the most elegant bird, but we need to maintain their habitats along their migrating path. The title is a play on the Isaac Watts lyrics, 'All the realms of nature mine'."

PLOVER

Above: Grey Plover – Robert Greenhalf (woodcut). Below: Ringed Plover, North Norfolk – Jeremy James (linocut).

GREY AND SILVER
BLOCK A of two blocks — Reduction block.

In order to get the solid blacks on the
face and underparts I have had to
cut overlays on top of the paper as
well as building up make-ready on
the back of the block to increase
the pressure in specific areas.

*Left: Grey and Silver – Thelma Sykes
(linocut). Above: block by Thelma
Sykes for 'Grey and Silver'.
Facing Page: A Stand of Plovers –
Lisa Hooper (collagraph).*

THERE ARE A NUMBER OF PLOVER species that either breed, over-winter or pass through the UK, with the most familiar being the Golden, Ringed, Little Ringed and Grey. Up to 60,000 pairs of Golden Plover breed on our shores, more than 5,000 pairs of Ringed Plover, and barely more than 1,000 pairs of Little Ringed Plover. In each case, substantially larger numbers of the birds over-winter in Britain. Not surprisingly, the artists have favoured the most widespread.

Thelma Sykes on the left depicts the Grey Plover, 70,000 of which pass through the UK in spring. Two blocks, one reduction, were used to create this print. "In order to get the solid blacks on the face and underparts, I have had to use overlays on top of the paper as well as building up make-ready on the back of the block to increase the pressure in specific areas."

Another reduction, or elimination,

print can be found on page 148 – representing a relatively rare deviation by Robert Gillmor. "The smart black-and-white head and chest pattern of Ringed Plovers, with plain ochre back and a zingy yellow-orange for beak and legs, allied with a neat, chunky shape, hold a special fascination for me. They have long been one of those birds that have no trouble finding their way into my sketchbooks.

"This quartet was brought together initially for a watercolour that included a mass of natural objects collected from Cley beach. The plovers formed a line across the top; and the shells, pebbles, seaweed, starfish, etc, spilled across the rest of the page. I thought the birds by themselves would make a workable subject for a linocut; and, as the colour range was small, an elimination print suggested itself."

Robert Greenhalf and Jeremy James open this section. The former has provided the woodcut of Grey Plovers on page 145 where the strong background colours set off well the more subdued plumage of the birds themselves. The linocut entitled 'Ringed Plover, North Norfolk' by Jeremy combines Sea Poppies with the characterful birds, scuttling among the coloured pebbles.

'A Stand of Plovers', above, by Lisa Hooper is a hand-coloured collagraph. "These Ringed Plovers were on the shore near my home in Port William, in south-west Scotland. They were perfectly camouflaged against the pebbles, a characteristic I wanted to

preserve. The wave in this print was crafted out of drizzled PVA: quite a playful process."

As with his Lapwings earlier in this book, Richard Jarvis's Golden Plovers linocut (left) is based on drawings done at Eyebrook Reservoir, using his car as a hide.

Peter Brown's wood engraving (above) features Ringed Plover. As a child, he played for hours on the seashore, "visiting favourite spots to watch barnacles, mussels, limpets and crabs. The small birds that spent their days along the same stretches were soon added to the list of things to be fascinated by. Behind the Ringed Plover in this engraving is a coastal vessel. Ships like this busily frequented the lough, and were watched with equal interest as they made their way to and from the Belfast docks."

Top: Ringed Plover Quartet – Robert Gillmor (linocut). Above: Golden Plovers – Richard Jarvis (linocut).
Above right: Ringed Plover – Peter Brown (wood engraving).

PUFFIN

Right: Puffins – Jane Smith (screenprint). Below: Thrifty Puffins – Vanna Bartlett (linocut).

A circus of Puffins

WE EXPECTED TO BE DELUGED WITH Puffin pictures, as everyone loves these colourful characters. Struggling in the UK as food sources dry up, they still nest in relatively large numbers, using abandoned rabbit holes or their own burrows excavated on grassy slopes.

Julie Orpen chose the collective noun 'Circus' for her puffin print on the left, reflecting their clown-like appearance.

"They are such lovable and comical birds: they have always been a firm favourite, and the collective noun suits perfectly," she says.

John Hatton's linocut below really emphasises that beak and the contrast with the black-and-white bodies. Jane Smith produced her screenprint on page 149 after joining scientists from the RSPB on Shetland to study Puffins. "We had been studying the birds because they were struggling to find enough sand eels to feed their chicks."

Skokholm Island is another prime location for puffin-watching, and inspired Julia Manning's print entitled 'Ravens' Nest' (opposite).

Vanna Bartlett points out that "a seabird colony is hardly a place for quiet contemplation, what with the constant comings and goings, the noise and the smell. When the assault on the senses almost overwhelms, I retreat from the cliff edge away from the maelstrom. Here amidst the clumps of Thrift is where you find the Puffin burrows. A favourite bird to sketch and ideally suited to a linocut print.

"My print 'Thrifty Puffins' [page 149] was printed from three blocks, but I also ran off a couple of black prints part way through cutting. I added a bit of colour to the birds and got two different prints, one bright and colourful and the other somewhat sombre [see 'On the Edge', right]. The two prints neatly encapsulate the way I feel when out sketching wildlife – the bright colour and joy of being out in the open air observing nature but tempered by the sobering thought that many species are facing difficult times with habitat loss and other pressures."

Facing page, top: A Circus of Puffins – Julie Orpen (linocut). Facing page, bottom: Puffins – John Hatton (linocut).
Below: Ravens' Nest – Julia Manning (woodcut). Bottom left: On the Edge – Vanna Bartlett (linocut). Bottom right: Puffins – Richard Allen (linocut).

RAZORBILL

ANOTHER AMBER-LISTED SEABIRD SPECIES, WITH APPROXIMATELY 130,000 breeding pairs in the UK. The remaining stronghold is northern Scotland, where large colonies still exist. There are none to be found nowadays between the Humber and the Isle of Wight.

This section is dominated by the Kittie Jones screenprint below right, inspired by a mixed media drawing made on the Isle of May when the artist was exploring the vertiginous cliffs that drop away to a vast stretch of water ending in the Bass Rock against the East Lothian coast. "The technique of screenprinting allowed me to explore flat shapes of colour to describe the open sea with softer, more drawn marks on top creating an interesting tension and allowing a more playful approach to the use of colour."

Lisa Hooper used the 'jigsaw' method for her print below. "A trip to the Isle of May several years ago gave me the opportunity to see a variety of auks and Puffins at close quarters. Starting out in a classic East Coast sea mist, the air suddenly cleared into a brilliant and sparkling summer's day. The sharp lines and markings of Razorbills

lend themselves to this sort of simplification. Jigsaw prints are another way of printing multiple colours in one pass, devised during the period when I only had an etching press. The plate is in effect cut into pieces, each one a different colour. These can be inked separately and arranged on the press bed prior to printing in one pass. The pieces leave a small white margin around them which is distinctive. I use children's foam sheets which are easy to cut, sometimes sticking some of them to a backing board if I can ink them together. I also make lino jigsaw prints, which do give you the extra advantage of being able to cut textures into them as well."

On the right is a single-block monochrome linocut print by Anne Townshend. She so enjoyed making a similar print of the Oystercatcher that she sought out other large black-and-white species as subjects for a family of linocuts.

Below left: A Summer's Day – Lisa Hooper (jigsaw print). Below: Razorbill – Kittie Jones (screenprint). Right: Razorbills – Anne Townshend (linocut).

RED-BREASTED GOOSE

A BIT OF AN INTRUDER, AS THE species does not breed in the UK and is only an occasional visitor to southern Britain. However, it is a favourite of many wildfowl collections and a particularly striking bird that migrates from the Siberian tundra.

Dating from 2004, this five-block linocut by Robert Gillmor captures a small and colourful goose that had long been on the list of 'walking linocuts' occupying the artist's crowded imagination. He became familiar with them during annual trips to the Martin Mere reserve to teach bird-sketching courses.

REDSHANK

Below: Redshanks – Kittie Jones (screenprint).

NO PRIZES HERE FOR GUESSING where the bird's name comes from. As well as the orange/red legs, the base of the bill is a match and goes rather well with the brown speckled back. An Amber-listed species, these waders can number 130,000 in winter, although the UK breeding total is nearer 25,000 pairs, occupying saltmarsh and flood meadows during the summer. The over-wintering birds appear largely from Iceland, and settle on estuaries and coastal lagoons.

Kittie Jones chose a screenprint for her image of Redshanks. "I was out drawing at the mouth of the River Esk which flows into the Firth of Forth. It was a crisp, winter day and a large group of Redshanks had been pushed up by the tide to rest in the sun underneath the sea wall. The light was a beautiful, soft yellow and this created strong harmonious colours which I built up with layers of hand-drawn marks in this screenprint [page 155]. The image came together with the last layer of a soft, translucent black."

Lisa Hooper's bird in 'Redshank, Stromness' (top right) was etched into

lino in a variation on the more familiar technique of cutting the material. "Lino can be etched – by which I mean the surface can be eaten away, using concentrated caustic soda. It is not a nice process, but it does create textures that would be difficult to achieve using linocutting tools. In this print you can see it on the rock surfaces. I use molten wax as a resist. The lino has a protective surface which has to be sanded off, and the caustic soda solution has to be left in place for some time depending on the temperature. The plate is carefully washed and brushed under running water to remove the softened lino. Extreme care should be taken with this method, and a proper set of instructions including health and safety advice used.

"This solitary bird was wandering around the shore of Hoy Sound near Stromness in the late afternoon. The still reflections, beautiful rockpools and soft light attracted me to the image."

Above, the same artist has reverted to a reduction linocut for the Redshanks at Girvan Harbour. "This rather quiet print evokes an equally quiet day birdwatching, with unglamorous birds

snoozing while the tide changes and a Mute Swan glides by. The backdrop is the harbour shuttering in Girvan, which reminds me of flock wallpaper."

Robert Greenhalf tackles the birds in flight with the woodcut print on the far left, showing the brilliant white trailing edge to the wing. Richard Allen included the linocut on the right in his *Coastal Birds* book, noting that the Redshank is often described as 'the sentinel of the marsh' as the bird is quick to sound the alarm at approaching danger.

Far left: Redshanks and Reeds – Robert Greenhalf (woodcut). Above centre: Girvan Harbour – Lisa Hooper (linocut). Above right: Redshank, Stromness – Lisa Hooper (etched linoprint). Right: Redshank – Richard Allen (linocut).

SANDERLING

Below: Racing the Waves – Nina Sage (linocut). Right: Sanderling print in progress. Far right: Sanderlings – Richard Allen (linocut).

THE AUTHOR OF THIS BOOK HAS BEEN collecting wildlife art for three decades; the very first original painting bought was of Sanderlings, so they have remained a favourite bird. In winter, they are most often seen racing along sandy beaches, feeding at the tideline – as shown on the left by Nina Sage.

"I have a soft spot for Sanderlings. They are such busy little birds, and I have enjoyed their company while beachcombing on a number of occasions. Their comical high speed shuttling to and fro at the tideline like clockwork toys always makes me smile, so I thought they would be an engaging subject for a linocut. It was a challenge to capture the energy of both their speedy scampering and the frothy lapping of the waves. I deliberately kept the sand smooth to contrast with the movement of the birds and the sea, adding interest with their reflections."

The image in the centre shows part of Nina's printmaking process. While her favourite method is linocutting, she prefers to use vinyl floor tiles, which take a fine line without crumbling in the press.

Richard Allen has also chosen the race along the wet sand for his Sanderlings linocut reproduced above. He enjoys the challenge of sketching and painting birds directly from life in the field in all weathers. The estuary of the River Colne near his home in Wivenhoe, Essex, provides plenty of inspiration, especially in winter when large numbers of waders and wildfowl flock to the coast.

SHAG

Below: Shag and Young – Kittie Jones (monotype).
Right: Shags – Carry Akroyd (serigraph).

RATHER OUTNUMBERED in this book by close cousin the Cormorant, the smaller and darker Shag can often be seen flying low over the water, but never flying in over land. Nest sites are inevitably on cliff ledges, making close observation a challenge. This is a Red-listed bird, with around 27,000 UK breeding pairs – but more than half the population is confined to fewer than 10 sites.

According to Kittie Jones, "Shags seem to lend themselves to the art of print. Something about the bold, unexpected shapes their bodies make combined with that distinctive black silhouette.

"This monotype [right] was made after drawing Shags with young on the Isle of May. I was interested in breaking down the image into planes of colour: the strong light on the adult bird's back allowed me to use the white of the paper to give structure; and the use of roller marks, combined with wipe marks, created a nice relationship between the graphic nature of the scene and a softer, more painterly approach."

Carry Akroyd's serigraph (screenprint) on the right was produced as an illustration for *Tweet of the Day*, published by John Murray. "I could choose 36 of the 240-something birds to feature as full colour pages, and in my mind's eye they all derived from some place where I had spent time watching that particular species. Much simplified, to me this is a particular rock favoured by Shags in the Isles of Scilly."

THERE IS A UK BREEDING population of 300,000-350,000 pairs of these Amber-listed seabirds, ungainly on land but spectacular when airborne. The adults leave their nest sites in July, abandoning their nestlings, to travel to the coast of South America, returning in February and March.

Offshore islands are the favoured breeding and nesting grounds, safe from predators such as rats. This Manx Shearwater and bluebell image ('Midnight Manxie', monoprint) is by Chris Wallbank, and is based on drawings made at night on Skomer Island. Skomer and Skokholm are between them home to more than half of the world's population of the species, nesting in burrows that the birds leave and enter only under the cover of darkness.

SHEARWATER

SHELDUCK

A BIG, COLOURFUL DUCK THAT IS A FAMILIAR SIGHT IN COASTAL locations as it grazes on invertebrates alongside waders. Around 15,000 pairs breed in the UK, with the winter population sometimes exceeding 80,000 birds.

'Shelduck Reflection' on the left is a linocut by John Hatton that emphasises that bold colour scheme – shared unusually by both duck and drake. This enabled Robert Gillmor to produce a 1998 linocut of a pair (far right) that for once gives both sexes equal billing.

Chris Sinden's 32-block linocut print below is typical of his style. After 30 years working as an advertising art director, redundancy convinced Chris that it was time for a career change. He decided to learn linocutting. But having come to the art relatively late in life, he was keen to find a style that would set his work apart. "Since those early experimental days I have developed a style where smaller images butt up to make the larger final picture. Utilising both printmaking techniques (one block, one colour and reduction printing), using slightly unmatched colours and details and often to an irregular format, most of my linocuts take on a collage appearance."

A white-line woodblock is the medium chosen by Lisa Hooper for her Shelduck work on the right. This watercolour technique – derived from Japanese woodblock printing – involves painting on to the block with a brush, and printing before the paint dries. "This print was made on quite a coarse-grained floor ply, which is visible in the finished image."

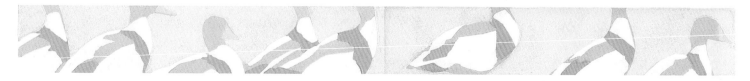

*Far left: Shelduck Reflection –
John Hatton (linocut). Bottom
left: Shelducks – Chris Sinden
(linocut). Right: Shelduck Pair
– Robert Gillmor (linocut). Far
right: Shelducks – Richard Allen
(linocut). Below: Shelduck – Lisa
Hooper (white-line woodblock).*

SHORELARK

THE SHORELARK IS A STRIKING SMALL bird found almost exclusively on the coast. In spite of the yellow/black colour scheme, it can be surprisingly hard to spot against coloured shingle on the beach. The feather tufts behind the eyes are responsible for the name Horned Lark. Whatever you choose to call this delightful bird, a sighting is likely to be elusive as over-wintering numbers vary between fifty and several hundred.

Robert Gillmor is responsible for the vibrant linocut print on the left, based clearly on birds visiting his local beach. "In winter plumage, which is how we mostly see them, this pattern is duller and the horns have gone. They are still striking and much sought after by birders along the shingle bank that borders the North Sea, a few minutes' walk from my studio. Here they may be found, along with drifts of Snow Buntings, two species that can brighten a chilly winter visit to the Norfolk coast."

Max Angus is a regular visitor to coastal north Norfolk, using her observations as the basis for linocut prints such as the one below, which also features Norfolk's visiting Pink-footed Geese. "Over the last few winters the Shorelarks have gathered at Holkham. They seem so bright and surreal with faces like yellow violas. They look like clowns dressed up to entertain. Winter cheerfulness."

Facing page: Shorelarks – Robert Gillmor (linocut). Below: Shorelarks and Pinkfeet – Max Angus (linocut).

SHOVELER

THESE SURFACE-FEEDING DUCKS ARE READILY identified by the spatulate bill, and can be found in large numbers during the winter when up to 20,000 birds can arrive on Britain's waterways. The UK breeding population is much smaller, estimated at 700-800 pairs, but Britain accounts for more than 20 per cent of the northwest European total. As with many wildfowl species, the ducks are rather less glamorous than the drakes, with a mottled brown colour scheme that makes them rather anonymous. Spring evenings can see pairs or small groups carrying out courtship flights at high speed, complete with aerobatic manoeuvres.

In Lisa Hooper's mixed media relief print to the right, a female joins the more decorative males. "This print was made using lino and cardboard plates. The key plate is printed in black and brown and is the last plate to be used." On page 168, the same artist has provided a hand-coloured etching of two drakes. "Shovelers have such a lot of character with their broad, powerful bills and squat stance – intent on shovelling! They are always in beautiful places where the soft sounds as the winter sun falls are the thing you really want to capture. The droplet of water on the bird's bill draws the eye."

Robert Greenhalf is responsible for the woodcut on the facing page, capturing ducks and drakes cruising the reedbed. Andrew Haslen has a soft spot for

*Facing page: Shovelers – Lisa Hooper
(mixed media, relief). Above right:
Shoveler – Andrew Haslen
(linocut). Right: Shovelers –
Robert Greenhalf (woodcut).*

Shovelers, having produced the hand-coloured linocut on the preceding page, as well as the Shoveler/Kingfisher combo reproduced here.

Robert Gillmor's five-block linocut from 2001 (right) shows the drake Shoveler reflecting its handsome plumage in still water. "It was not this gorgeous outfit that I was after in this little print. It was almost a lino sketch, and slightly experimental, as I worked out a treatment for the reflection. It took five blocks: black; chestnut and yellow for the bird; with two tones of green for the surround."

Above: Shovelers – Lisa Hooper (etching). Above right: Shoveler and Kingfisher – Andrew Haslen (linocut). Right: Drake Shoveler – Robert Gillmor (linocut).

SKUA

Below: Biscay Bonxie I – Chris Wallbank (monotype).

Right: Chris Wallbank pulling 'Biscay Bonxie IV'. Far right: Biscay Bonxie IV – Chris Wallbank (monotype). Below: Great Skua – Peter Brown (wood engraving).

GREAT SKUAS, ALSO KNOWN AS Bonxies, are piratical birds of the high seas, stealing food from Gannets and killing more lovable birds such as Puffins. They have little fear of humans, attacking with vigour if you get too close to the nesting site. Bonxies migrate from their wintering grounds in Spain and Africa to the most northerly islands of the UK. Approximately 10,000 pairs can nest in Britain, and the birds are most likely to be spotted here between April and July.

Peter Brown's wood engraving below shows the heavy, short-tailed bird in typical breeding habitat, patrolling the cliffs on the lookout for fish it can steal or vulnerable birds it can attack. "I chose to reflect some of this bird's reputed character by composing the picture so that it would fly in front of a tall and menacing cliff, made more forbidding by being largely in shadow. Behind the skua at the foot of the cliff, small seabirds fly quickly away."

Chris Wallbank's two Bonxie prints are based on observations made from a ferry crossing the Bay of Biscay. The artist can be seen on the right pulling the large and impressive watercolour monotype print that dominates this section. "Watercolour monotypes are made by applying watercolour paint to a plastic plate, which is then pressed on to wet paper. I use several plates on one print to build up layers of colour." The previous image on page 169 is another watercolour monotype by Chris, entitled 'Biscay Bonxie I'.

A Red conservation status bird, the

Above: components of Lisa Hooper's Arctic Skua jigsaw print. Left: Arctic Skua, Orkney – Lisa Hooper (jigsaw print).

Arctic Skua depicted here by Lisa Hooper does breed in the UK (just over 2,000 pairs) but can generally be seen only in the Shetland and Orkney island groups, occasionally on northern Scottish coastal moorlands. A more elegant bird than the Great Skua, it targets terns and gulls for food theft, so is often spotted around northern tern colonies. Lisa used her jigsaw print method for the Arctic Skua print on the left, with the component parts of the block reproduced above.

"This jigsaw print is on lino which enabled me to cut textures into some of the pieces so that the light on the sea could be described. The view is looking south down the coast from Yesnaby towards Hoy, with the Old Man visible in the distance. Arctic Skuas and Bonxies both patrol this coast during the summer months."

Smew

SUCH A STRIKING BIRD, THE SMEW IS A SMALL diving duck that over-winters in the UK in small numbers (generally up to 200), having left the colder climes of Russia and Scandinavia. It is a relatively mysterious species, given the harsh and remote location of its breeding grounds. The male is particularly splendid with his black mask and back. The female is attractive in her own right, although often confused with the Goldeneye. The male in eclipse looks much more like his mate, regaining full plumage in late autumn.

John Hatton to the right offers us his linocut 'Smew Parade' that emphasises the monotone style of the drake birds. Thelma Sykes is responsible for the other two prints in this section plus a preparatory sketch from 1997 that helped

Above right: Smew Parade – John Hatton (linocut).
Below: preparatory Smew sketch by Thelma Sykes.
Right: Smew – Thelma Sykes (linocut).

in the creation of the linocuts shown here.

"It has great presence, the Smew, despite its small size; and the drake, with clear-cut, cracked ice markings, is a gift to a printmaker. I am well placed to see Smew in the winter, since I am not far from the Shropshire Meres, but I did most of the drawing of one individual at Burton Mere on the Dee Estuary just a short distance from my home. He returned over six consecutive winters. My linocut 'Smew' [page 173] is an unashamed celebration of pattern, but I also want to show that the Smew are alerted by something beyond the picture format and might fly, or dive, at any moment. I crop the crest of the upper Smew to bring the focus close and to add to the tension."

The print on the left is entitled 'Icebreaker' and was commissioned as a cover for *Wildfowl and Wetlands Winter 1997*. "The Smew toughs out the harshest of our winters yet it looks delicate – and it is very small. For a few years a superb drake Smew wintered on my local patch giving plenty of scope for study. With its black-and-white plumage and crisp-cut lines, this charismatic duck is made to be celebrated in linocut.

"The structure of the composition came from a very different place, Loch Garten, late October, and very (very) cold. The far side of the loch was scored by a band of intense white, more vibrant than any other reflection. Only later did I understand what I had drawn when I followed the Mallachie track: the waters on the far side were frozen. A wide shelf of ice followed the contours of the shore, trapped around the stems of the emerging vegetation. That moment of understanding gave me the horizontal division of the picture space that underpins the composition of 'Icebreaker', and the colour reflects the golden/ochre of winter larch with hints of green and red from pine and birch gleaming through."

Left: Icebreaker – Thelma Sykes (linocut).

SNIPE

BLESSED WITH SHORT LEGS AND VERY LONG bills, Snipe are pretty unmistakeable waders that breed in relatively large numbers in the UK, but where the population is dwindling. In winter, there can be upwards of a million birds visiting waterlogged vegetation on the hunt for invertebrates.

Chris Sinden's 25-block linocut below right was compiled from three references. "The Snipe wasn't standing next to the marsh-marigold at Slimbridge; the background wasn't at Slimbridge, either. The marigold was growing near the upper reaches of the River Brede in East Sussex; and the tangled background was inspired by a stream bank several fields away from where I discovered the marigold. The look of the print was important, so I challenged my ability to print the Snipe and the marigold as a cutout against the background."

"Snipe are so shy and elusive," explains Lisa Hooper. "It makes them quite hard to observe closely. These two [on page 177] were in our local nature reserve at Wigtown, which fortunately has a hide. This print has been printed in a very dark brown with dabs of black ink on the eyes. This technique of applying different colours to the plate in different areas is borrowed from etching and is known as à la poupée. It has been hand coloured afterwards in watercolour."

Right: Snipe – Richard Jarvis (linocut). Below: Snipe sketch by Richard Jarvis. Far right: Marigold Snipe – Chris Sinden (linocut). Page 176: Three Snipe – Andrew Haslen (linocut). Page 177: Snipe – Lisa Hooper (linocut).

S TILT

THE ELUSIVE BLACK-WINGED STILT IS A SOMEWHAT UNGAINLY WADER THAT is a relatively rare visitor to the UK and an occasional British breeder. There were numerous sightings in the Norfolk Broads in 2018, resulting in a considerable increase in visitor numbers to the wader-rich waterlogged meadows near Martham. In 2017, an unprecedented 13 chicks fledged in Britain, at sites in Cambridgeshire, Kent and Norfolk. Thelma Sykes first saw the bird in May 1987, at Holme in Norfolk. Her print, below, came 14 years later, after she had more experience of the species, having met a famous stilt that visited Druridge Bay, Northumberland, in July 1993, moved after two weeks to Snettisham in Norfolk and then found a home at the nearby Titchwell RSPB reserve. "Here he stayed for 12 years, and became known as Sammy."

S WAN

Below left: Swan, Kew Gardens – Mike Smith (linocut). Below centre: Black Swan – Andy English (wood engraving). Below right: Swan – Sue Brown (collagraph).

WHOOPER, BEWICK'S, MUTE AND BLACK Swans occupy these pages, mixing the genuinely wild with the obviously cultivated. Like the poor, Mute Swans are always with us. They prosper ornamentally on ponds, lakes, rivers, along coasts and in estuaries. An unhealthy diet augmented by chips, white bread and corn sold as duck food doesn't seem to do them much harm, although anglers' lead fishing weights and abandoned line have resulted in many casualties.

Britain provides a winter home for the rarer Whooper and Bewick's. The former is the bigger of the two wild species, with more yellow on its bill and a distinctive voice. They arrive with us in varying numbers during October to November, departing for more northerly climes in March/April. Young Bewick's accompany the adults on their annual migration from the Arctic tundra, via the Baltic to western Europe. As with the Whoopers, we rejoice in their autumn arrival at our reserves and other roosting/grazing grounds.

The single image of the Australian Black Swan here (below centre) is courtesy of Ely wood engraver Andy English. These birds are an ornamental feature of many private collections, but some made their escape to join Mute Swans and various ducks on our waterways. "I love to watch the stately glide of a swan along a waterway. We live quite close to the Welney Wetland Centre where early morning feeding and sunset arrivals can be spectacular. The bird I finally engraved was a Black Swan I saw on the River Cam in Cambridge. I was as fascinated by the shape of the displaced water as by the bird itself."

Encounters with Mute Swans can be uncomfortable, as these are big birds and can sometimes be aggressive. Caroline Barker contributed 'Swanning About' on page 183. "We do a lot of canoeing on our estuary and have encountered a very bad-tempered swan that would fly straight at our canoe; so, when we could, we turned about. We always give

A lamentation of swans

the swans a wide berth now, hence them being a bit farther away in the print."

Julie Orpen also chose Mute Swans as a linocut subject (above), allocating the collective noun 'lamentation' for the birds. "This was chosen as I have often enjoyed visiting the large gatherings of majestic swans along the river bank at Mistley in Essex featured in the background of the print."

Sue Brown is an artist who uses printmaking to tell stories. Her work springs from the pages of her sketchbook, and she develops carefully researched

themes, experimenting with collagraph printmaking with which she explores the relationships we have with our feathered friends; she is fascinated by all things ornithological. Living in Gloucestershire gives Sue easy access to Slimbridge Wetland Centre when inspiration is sought, resulting in prints such as the swan collagraph on page 179.

Mike Smith's Mute Swan on page 179 was seen at Kew Gardens. "A languid, sultry day with hardly a breath of air. The swan floated on the pond, occasionally dipping its beak into the still waters. As it raised its head

Facing page: Whooper Swans and Pochard – Robert Greenhalf (woodcut). Above: A Lamentation of Swans – Julie Orpen (linocut).

Above left: The Bewicks are Back – Robert Gillmor (linocut).
Above centre: Swanning About – Caroline Barker (linocut).
Above right: One Swan – Nick Wonham (linocut).
Left: Lode Swans – Valerie Sims (woodcut).

a drip would fall from its beak, and I was fascinated to see that, owing to the stillness and tension of the water surface, a bubble would form and remain, at least until the swan dipped its head again."

'One Swan', the linocut on the far right, is by Nick Wonham. "Reflections can become an important pictorial device in prints of water birds, and this is certainly true of 'One Swan'. I like the way the orange beak stands out against the dark green water; and the horizontal axis of the neck and its reflection, along with the horizontal ripples, creates a sense of serenity."

'Lode Swans' on the left is by Valerie Sims. "On a very cold December morning, I came upon these swans and young on the edge of Wicken Lode. I like the way they tuck their beaks

under their wings, except for the cob on this occasion, who was keeping his eye on me."

Turning to wild swans, the woodcut on page 180 by Robert Greenhalf combines Whoopers and the rather attractive Pochard. "Sketching Whooper Swans from a centrally heated hide at Welney, I liked the contrast in scale between the huge sedate swans and the much smaller Pochards diving amongst them." The same artist mixes Bewick's Swans with Pintails in the woodcut reproduced on page 184.

For Robert Gillmor's 2017 Christmas card of returning Bewick's Swans "I decided on quite a straightforward print [above left] with only three blocks. Rather than have a fourth block, it was simpler to paint the yellow on the swans' beaks. I used the water-based printing ink that is comparatively light-fast for a fugitive colour like yellow. I was late (as usual!) preparing this design, and more than grateful to the printer for rushing it through."

On page 184, Lisa Hooper's reduction

linocut is of Whooper Swans. "These swans, backlit against winter sun, were at the Crook of Baldoon, our local RSPB reserve close to Wigtown in Dumfries and Galloway. A new reserve, it already attracts good numbers of wintering Whoopers."

Also found overleaf is a majestic serigraph by Carry Akroyd entitled 'The Swans Return to the Loch' that she produced in 2011 and also features in our book of Carry's work, *Found in the Fields* (Mascot Media, 2017).

Top left: Bewick's Swans and Pintails – Robert Greenhalf (woodcut). Above: Whooper Swans – Lisa Hooper (linocut).
Right: The Swans Return to the Loch – Carry Akroyd (serigraph).

TERN

BRITAIN PLAYS HOST TO A NUMBER OF tern species. Here we reproduce prints of the Little Tern, Sandwich Tern and Common Tern, while fans of the Arctic Tern can admire the late Greg Poole's 'Arctic Terns and Ringed Plover' monoprint on page 2.

There are Little Tern colonies near us in Norfolk, with RSPB wardens patrolling the beach near Winterton-on-Sea to keep people, dogs and predatory Kestrels away from nesting parents and chicks. It is wonderful watching these tiny birds diving off the east coast.

Kerry Buck is a Norfolk-based printmaker, and she also has been charmed by these Amber-listed visitors that breed in relatively small numbers (no more than 2,000 pairs) on our shores. Her collagraph print is at the top of this spread. "These birds have such a great shape, all angles and sharp points. The pebbles were created by dribbling various substances across printer paper and then cutting out the shapes and collaging them to the board. The slightly raised surface leaves a fine black line around the pebble which is very effective."

Above is another image of Little Terns, this time by Lisa Hooper who used her mixed media relief printing method. "Inspired by Little Terns on South Ronaldsay, Orkney, this print was made using two cardboard plates and one woodcut. One plate was used to print the sand, one had foam pieces stuck to it and was used to print the grey wings of the birds, and the last plate (the wooden one) provided the black outlines and was used with silver paper for the chine-collé sand eel."

A woodcut of Little Terns waiting at the

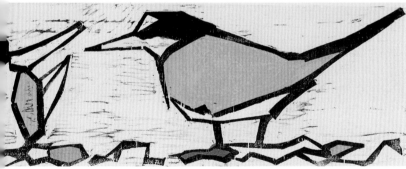

Top: Little Terns – Kerry Buck (collagraph). Above: Little Terns – Lisa Hooper (mixed media relief print). Left: Three Terns – Nick Wonham (linocut/woodcut). Right: Common Tern – Richard Allen (linocut).

tideline has been provided by Robert Greenhalf on page 190.

The Common Tern featured in prints by Nick Wonham (page186) and Richard Allen (page 187) has the nickname 'Sea Swallow', thanks to its long tail and graceful flight. Floating platforms complete with sand and

shingle are provided on some inland waterways such as the Norfolk Broads to help attract these birds and encourage them to nest. While named 'common', there are only about 12,000 nesting pairs in the UK.

Nick Wonham encountered his birds in the Farne Islands. "A few years ago we visited

Northumberland and took a boat tour around the Farne Islands, specifically to see Puffins. But it was the striking lighthouse, with its red and white stripes, and the terns that ended up inspiring my 'Three Terns' print. The yellow is printed from a piece of plywood, while the rest of it is printed from lino. The ink printed from

Left: Sandwich Terns – Lisa Hooper (woodcut). Right: New Arrivals – Robert Greenhalf (woodcut).

the rough ply was so textured I could hardly print over it, and only ended up with a very small edition."

Thanks perhaps to a fancy hairdo, the Sandwich Tern has been a popular choice with our artists. Similar numbers to the Common Tern breed in the UK, but they are highly dependent on our nature reserves for secure nesting sites.

Robert Greenhalf, based in East Sussex and close to the Kent border, explains that he always awaits eagerly the arrival of the first Sandwich Terns in March on the south coast, as evidenced by his woodcut print above entitled 'New Arrivals'.

Lisa Hooper is responsible for the reduction woodcut opposite. "This woodcut was made using floor ply, and the grain is clearly visible. I used a dabber to apply the

Left: To the Sea – Robert Greenhalf (woodcut). Top: Little Terns – Robert Greenhalf (woodcut). Above: Sandwiches on the Beach – Lisa Hooper (linocut).

soft shadows in the white bodies of the birds before cutting anything away. These breeding birds were at Minsmere in Suffolk, although we do see adults fishing in the summer on the Galloway coast." Above, the same artist produced this reduction linocut entitled 'Sandwiches on the Beach'. "This slightly light-hearted print was made after seeing breeding Sandwich Terns at Minsmere. The pebbles were inspired by 1960s wallpaper."

TUFTED DUCK

A MUCH-LOVED SPECIES OF DIVING DUCK, where the drake is once again a favourite of printmakers thanks to colour, shape and the drooping crest that gives the bird its name. More than 100,000 birds can over-winter in the UK, while up to 19,000 pairs breed in Britain.

John Hatton's linocut of two Tufted drakes (top left) captures the yellow eye and the striking bill colour. Chris Sinden (above) uses a 32-block linocut to illustrate the same subject, while Janice Earley on the left favours a raft of the male birds in her linocut. They take to open waters in large flocks during the winter, visiting harbours and sea bays as well as lakes and ponds.

Top left: Tufted Drakes – John Hatton (linocut).
Top right: Tufted Ducks – Chris Sinden (linocut).
Left: Tufted Ducks – Janice Earley (linocut).

WHIMBREL

Below: Whimbrel – Peter Brown (wood engraving).
Bottom: Whimbrel – Kerry Buck (collagraph).

BREEDING LARGELY IN NORTHERN SCOTLAND, THE WHIMBREL IS SEEN elsewhere in the UK while on passage during the spring and autumn as the bird migrates to and from Africa. The conservation status is Red, given the breeding population of no more than 500 pairs and the limited sites in Orkney and Shetland.

Kerry Buck produced the collagraph below. "I found great satisfaction in creating the water by dribbling Hammerite and PVA glue in swirling patterns, using this texture as the water and the basis of the final composition. I was lucky enough to spot two of these birds on a visit to Walberswick in Suffolk, thinking they were Curlew until a more knowledgeable gentleman pointed out the distinguishing white line behind their eyes."

Peter Brown first remembers seeing Whimbrel while on holiday in the Yorkshire Dales. "It was during nesting season, and walkers were being warned lest we disturb a nest or crush an egg. These two I have brought south to an estuary just north of the Thames, where I have seen them feeding on the mud flats and tidal creeks."